**Foreword By
Bishop Emmanuel Louis Nterful**

Pursuing
GOD
In Your Difficult Times

Emmanuel Obed Quao

Address
Rev'd Fr Emmanuel Obed Nii Otu Quao
C/o Anglican Diocese of Accra
Bishop's Court.
GP 8 Accra
+233 24 114 4202
doxaobed@yahoo.com

Cover design by Xpertmindz Ent.
Tel: 024 469 9777

CONTENTS

DEDICATION

To

Joseline, my life's companion; and our children, Eliana and Christos

ACKNOWLEDGMENT

Deep appreciation goes to my Lord Bishop, The Rt. Rev'd. Dr Daniel Sylvanus Mensah Torto and Rt. Rev'd Dr. George Kotei Neequaye, for their unreserved support and encouragement.

An unreserved gratitude goes to Very Rev'd Samuel Hansen Addy and Canon Samuel Ankrah for recommending me to the Diocese to begin my priestly formation. I appreciate the financial support of Rev'd Fr. Samuel Quartey, who raised funds at Holy Family Church, Adenta, to support my ministry when I was posted to Otinibi.

I received invaluable support from the members of the Guild of Good Shepherd of Christ Church, Legon, during my transfer to Otinibi. In particular, I would like to thank Dr. Sarah Akrofi Quarcoo, Madam Alfreda Quaye, and Mrs. Georgina Quartey. May God bless each of you abundantly.

I am deeply grateful for the overwhelming support and contributions recieved from friends and other parishioners during our fundraising and harvest activities. Your generousity has been instrumental in our success

I am also grateful to all who invited me to speak at revivals, retreats and all nights programmes, and particularly for their encouragement. I am grateful to God for the entire membership of St. Michael- Korle Gonno (Home Parish), St. Mary the Virgin - Accra, Holy Family - Adenta, St. Christopher - Otinibi, St. Barnabas - Osu, SS Peter & Paul - Kwabenya, St. Andrew - Abossey Okai and St. Francis of Assisi - Mamprobi.

My thanks also go to my Parish Priest, Rev'd Fr. Roland Kpoanu, for his support and encouragement. And to the entire clergy of the Anglican Church of Ghana.
I also appreciate the good work of Gifty E. Annan-Myers, who proofread the manuscript.

My mother, Gertrude Otoo, my sister, Mrs. Sandra Laryea, and my family, I pray for God's continued blessings.
To my ministerial colleagues, friends, spiritual sons and daughters, Miracle Wave Ministry Group, and to all who have made an impact on my life and supported my ministry, God richly bless you. I also owe an inestimable debt to my wife, for her encouragement.

Finally, I thank God for His favour upon my life and ministry, and I continue to ask Him to keep me faithful through his amazing grace.

Nevertheless, human error is always possible, hence, I accept responsibility for any flaws in this book.

PRAISE FOR THE BOOK

We are bound to face challenges in life. It's part of human existence. However, once we have Jesus on our side, we can navigate through life's challenges with ease. This is what the author has elaborated on in this book. It's my prayer that by reading it, no matter what you encounter, heavenly visitation will be experienced.
Rev'd Canon Patrick Okaijah-Bortier PhD
Parish Priest, St Andrew Anglican Church, Abossey Okai,
The President, Global Revival Theological College.

Life complexities are not mere obstacles but components of personal growth and resilience. Pursuing God in Your Difficult Times is a must-read for anyone seeking to understand the purpose behind life struggles—and find strength in adversity. The book is a timely resource for everyone seeking to have a deeper relationship with God.
Rev'd Dr. Abraham Boateng
Lecturer, Trinity Theological Seminary, Legon

During times of strain, it is often not easy to cope—because it is not an experience devoid of pain. But having our living faith in Him and knowing He will never leave us shall be enough to get us through our trials. Our suffering on earth is a small price to pay for the vast riches and glory that await us. He knows that by allowing us to experience breakdown and pain, we will grow stronger in our faith, become closer to Him, and move away from sin. God does not cause us misery, but He can and may allow it to accomplish something good for us.

"Be strong and of good courage, do not fear nor be afraid of them: for the LORD your God, He is the One who goes with you. He will not leave you, nor forsake you." (Deut 31:6)

Lay Canon Michael N.A. Cobblah, *Investment Banker, C.E.O. & Co-Founder of C-NERGY Global Holdings PTY*

Amid life's inevitable challenges, Pursuing God in Your Difficult Times offers a profound exploration of spiritual resilience and divine providence. Through insightful reflections, this book illuminates the transformative journey of recognizing suffering as a catalyst for character development and a deeper connection with God. With wisdom and compassion, it guides readers through the storms of life, inspiring faith, resilience, and a renewed sense of purpose. Discover the transformative power of embracing challenges as pathways to divine love and spiritual refinement in Pursuing God in Your Difficult Times.

Lay Canon Dr. Emmanuel N. A. Tackie, CGIA, JP
Lead Consultant- D2E Consulting Ltd

In the journey of life, we all encounter storms that test the very fabric of our being. This book is a beacon of light amidst life's tempests. Through poignant anecdotes and profound insights, this book guides us through the tumultuous seas of hardship, offering solace, wisdom, and a renewed sense of purpose. Drawing from personal experiences and timeless biblical truths, the author eloquently reminds us that while adversity may be inevitable, defeat is not predetermined. With unwavering faith as our compass, we navigate the darkest nights, knowing that dawn will inevitably break. As a minister who has weathered his storms, the author's words resonate with authenticity and empathy. From the barren landscapes of doubt to the fertile valleys of hope, this book charts a course toward spiritual resilience and unwavering trust in the divine.

'Pursuing God in difficult times' is not merely a book; it is a lifeline for the soul-weary and the heartbroken. It reminds us that in the crucible of adversity, our faith is refined, and our spirits are strengthened. I wholeheartedly recommend this book to all who seek solace, guidance, and a steadfast anchor amid life's storms."

Alfred Amoah

Managing Director Bloom Bank Africa

We would all be richer in understanding if we spent time reading and re-reading Pursuing God in Your Difficult Times. *It is full of insights and guidance from the Bible with practical experiences tailored to assist us during our periods of hardships and challenges. This process eventually, refines and molds us into better persons.*

Mr. Eddie Otoo

Priest Warden Pro-Cathedral/ Management Consultant

In these challenging times of economic and social adversity, the most invaluable guidance one can receive is the counsel to seek God. Reverend Father Obed Quao has admirably conveyed this message in his book. Utilizing biblical verses, scriptural examples, and real-life scenarios, he adeptly demonstrates the imperative of placing unwavering trust in God, irrespective of the difficulties or trials one may encounter.

I fervently endorse "Pursuing God in Difficult Times" as essential reading. This book is not only for Christians or those currently facing hardships but for anyone who desires to witness firsthand the profound power and love of God.

Dr. Nathaniel Tetteh

Reconstructive and Plastic surgeon (Trauma and specialist Hospital) and People's Warden (St. Andrew Anglican Church)

PURSUING GOD IN YOUR DIFFICULT TIMES *clearly underscores the imperativeness of prayer in the life of a Christian. That we should approach our difficulties with a spirit of perseverance and prayer, knowing that every challenge is an opportunity for God to work in our lives. We unreservedly recommend this book to you to read and get copies for others.*
Mr. Carl Clottey & Family

Pursuing God in Your Difficult Times is a must-read for anyone that needs a reference book for their difficult time. The book, using various Bible stories, illustrates how difficult times are temporary phases in the life that God has planned for us. They are inevitable. How we overcome them is through our faith and by forgiving those who wrong us. The story of Joseph is strongly featured throughout the book to illustrate how we are elevated in God's heart and rewarded when we forgive those who wrong us. All Bible references are excellently researched.
Gifty E. Annan-Myers

It is written in the Scriptures, "In this world you will have tribulations" (John16:33). The road of life is full of speed bumps and potholes. We all struggle with different issues in life, and rather than pursuing God for answers, we run away from God. Rev'd Fr. Emmanuel Obed Quao, in this book, has given us reasons why we go through suffering and tribulations in this world and why it is important to pursue God amid adversity. He outlines that God uses our troubles and sufferings to help us help others in similar situations. The reader will find out as Rev'd Fr. Quao puts it "setbacks are not the end of a journey but rather part of the journey." No matter how painful the situation may be, the writer makes us understand that God can use our trials and tribulations to our advantage. So, he encourages that one can still pursue God in the course of suffering and pain because it is in God that we find strength to face the affairs of life. I urge you to read this book with an open mind and note the importance of being a pursuer of God in your most difficult circumstances.

Rev'd Stella Blankson-Cann
CEO/ PRESIDENT of Stella Blankson -Cann Ministries Intn'l

"Tough times don't last, but tough people do," and they only do it successfully in pursuance of the Great One. The opening chapters of the book Pursuing God in Your Difficult Times aptly admit the reality that difficult times are an integral part of human life. The writer succeeds in using personal life experiences to illustrate how a believer can seamlessly navigate tough times by pursuing God.

I recommend this book to especially our teaming youth and the younger generation to arm themselves with the insights and tools provided as the most potent antidote for combatting the perilous times ahead of their live journey.

Sally Amaki Darko Attopee (Mrs)
Consultant (CENDLOS)
Headmistress, Holy Trinity Cathedral SHS

FOREWORD

As Christians, we cannot prevent or avoid challenges, difficulties, problems, temptations, disappointments, failures, and the like. They are an inexorable part of our earthly life and walk with the Lord. The scriptures are clear on this.

"Man that is born of a woman Is of few days, and full of trouble" (Job 14:1
"Many are the afflictions of the righteous: but the LORD delivereth him out of them all" (Psalms 34:19).

"Good people might have many problems, but the Lord will take them all away" (Psalms 34:19 ERV).
"We are troubled on every side, yet not distressed; we are perplexed, but not in despair; Persecuted, but not forsaken; cast down, but not destroyed (2 Corinthians 4:8-9).

Notice what happens to us…afflictions, troubles, perplexity, persecution, rejection, and so on.

In PURSUING GOD IN YOUR DIFFICULT TIMES, Rev Emmanuel Obed Quao encourages us not to give up during such times. Rather, he teaches us to understand why such moments happen in our lives and the need for us to run to the Lord for help. He ably demonstrates to us that such challenges will pass if we put our trust in the Lord.

The Psalmist affirms these positions:

"I waited patiently for the Lord to help me, and he turned to me and heard my cry. He lifted me out of the pit of despair, out of the mud and the mire. He set my feet on solid ground and steadied me as I walked along. He has given me a new song to sing, a hymn of praise to our God. Many will see what he has done and be amazed. They will put their trust in the Lord" (Psalms 40:1-3NLT)

None of these things must move us! (Acts 20:22-24). We must not despair, be perplexed, and feel forsaken! (2 Cor. 4:8-10). Rather, we must take the issues to God through prayer and intercession and trust Him to see us through them (Psalm 42:5, Phil 4:6). Like King David, we must seek and pursue God in such difficult times (1 Samuel 30:8; Psalm 121).

In this world of relentless confusion, perplexity, poverty, disease, bereavement, marital disharmony, and the like, PURSUING GOD IN YOUR DIFFICULT TIMES could not have been inspired and written at a better time! I highly recommend this book to all believers, and in fact, all humanity.

Thank you, Rev Emmanuel Obed Quao, for showing us what to do in our difficult times.

BISHOP DR EMMANUEL LOUIS NTERFUL,
MD, MA IN MISSIOLOGY (Research);
Resident Bishop, Anagkazo Assemblies, UD-OLGC, KASOA, ACCRA, GHANA;
VICE-CHANCELLOR, ANAGKAZO BIBLE AND MINISTRY TRAINING CENTER, AKWAPIMG MAMPONG, ACCRA, GHANA;
FORMER CONVENOR, THE UNITED DENOMINA-

TIONS ORIGINATING FROM THE LIGHTHOUSE
GROUP OF CHURCHES (UD-OLGC);
CONVENOR, CHURCH GROWTH CONFERENCE,
GHANA.

INTRODUCTION

Facing adversity or difficult times tends to be a common challenge that all of us have to deal with every now and then.
As real as difficult times are, no one has ever mastered them. They remain an unconquered aspect of our lives, even for the most clever or smartest people.
Difficult times remain seasons in our life we never look forward to because we don't find them pleasant.

Hardships come in many forms. They come in the form of temptations, illnesses, unemployment, broken relationships, or persecution as a people of faith. They are an enemy with different colours and shape.

Adversities or difficult times manifest as "tribulation, or distress, or persecution, or famine, or nakedness, or danger, or sword?" (Romans 8:35, ESV). They are an inevitable part of our experience and a reality shared by everyone alive, Christian or otherwise.

As Christians, if we become equipped with the understanding of the workings of our faith, we will not be caught off guard when confronted by hardship.
By a better understanding of what Christ has called us to, we know that difficult times are part and parcel of our life and should be an anticipated component of our faith.

A good number of us are familiar with periods of trouble and turmoil in our lives. We grapple with personal traumas such as the loss of loved ones, deteriorating health, unemployment, divorce, instances of violent crime, and tragic accidents.

Our world appears to be caught in one crisis after another. The erstwhile worldwide pandemic has reshaped our daily lives and introduced major changes to our norms. Economic instability, political unrest, and social upheaval have further compounded the challenges we face, complemented by numerous natural disasters.

In my own life, I have had many experiences that relate to the subject matter of this book—pursuing God amidst life's challenges. In my own difficult times, I have had to ask the same questions that people ask when they go through difficult times.

In August 2016, I was appointed to serve as a priest in-charge of St. Christopher Anglican Congregation ,Otinibi. At that time, Otinibi was a newly developing community. The church was a modest initiative—an incomplete structure of a worship place, and membership predominantly comprising Sunday school children, and a handful of adults.

I realized I had to start from scratch, establishing a foundation upon which to build. It was one of the most difficult moments of my priestly ministry..

To make matters worse, there were two other separate congregations that were added to my responsibility.
They were the St. Philip and the St. Monica congregations, located at Kweiman and Danfa respectively. We coined the term "Churches on the Lane" to describe these three churches,

all of which were struggling to grow at the time. For some time, I serves as priest of all three congregations until a priest was brought to relieve me of my charge of the Kweiman and Danfa congregations. Handling these three churches alone further compounded my challenges as a young inexperienced priest.

In all, my wife and I spent two years with the St. Christopher congregation, and by the end of the period, we had achieved a marvelous work. We gradually assembled the necessary components. By the time my tenure drew to a close, our efforts had culminated in the dedication of a church building, fully-fledged place of worship. We were also able to put up a structure for the children's service department and undertook a lot of other things. Our endeavor commenced with minimal resources, yet through concerted efforts, we achieved comprehensive completion.

Irrespective of the origins of these challenging periods that cause disruptions to our lives, facing them takes a huge toll on our emotional state, physical well-being, and general perspective on things. As part of life's trials, we will experience sadness, feelings of betrayal, or even anger. These emotional responses do not necessarily amount to sin—unless we permit them to take root and grow and bear negative fruits.

The experience can cause a sense of helplessness and hopelessness, accompanied by levels of emotional strain or pressure. We constantly have reasons to grieve as we have to contend with painful situations and grapple with uncertainty regarding the choices we have to make. We may have fear regarding what to expect in our relationships or marriage, academic endeavours or career, all of which breed sorrow.

We can't avoid difficult times and the sorrows that accompany them. Yet by the grace of God, we can find our way out of them effectively and take charge of our life. We can develop the capacity to confront and endure every form of loss, change, and trauma. God has put in us the capacity to adapt to these challenges, navigate boisterous periods, and recover from them.

Difficulties will face all of us. But there is a way God wants us to handle things. The problem is that many of us Christians do not know what to do with our difficult times. We fail to handle them properly because we lack a proper approach to navigating through them. For such, I recommend the Bible.

The Bible provides a discerning perspective on how to effectively handle difficult times. It helps us understand God's perspective of our challenges, and better positions us to cope with them.

The insights and guidance that the Bible furnishes us with are tailored to assist us during our periods of hardship. In the scriptures, God outlines specific approaches by which He desires us to confront our challenges. His intention is for our relationship with Him to endure difficult times. Knowing that the biggest danger posed by difficult times is the possibility of our attitudes and sentiments toward Him changing, His main concern is to safeguard against any such possible change in our hearts as a result of our difficult times.

As we will discover in this book, some people do not recover from their difficult times. Their difficult times tend to become insurmountable obstacles that lead to their ultimate downfall. In the face of adversity, they forsake their allegiance to God and turn their backs on Him for good.

But the Bible encourages us to rather pursue God in our difficult moments.

We are to pursue Him just as we pursue our goals and objectives in life—such as seeking higher education, pursuing a promotion, enhancing our quality of life, managing physical fitness, and seeking companionship through marriage.

Our pursuit of these objectives in life is marked by a strong desire to attain our goals, regardless of the duration or challenges associated with the pursuit. God wants us to apply more, if not the same efforts we put into pursuing our earthly aspirations, to the pursuit of our relationship with Him as well as all matters pertaining to Him. When we prioritize the pursuit of God, it results in the fulfillment of our other aspirations.
The attainment of our other objectives becomes notably more feasible when God is placed at the forefront of our endeavors.

In the midst of adversity, when we are faced with challenging circumstances, God wants us to make Him our goal and topmost priority. He wants us to draw closer to Him so that He can carry or offload our burden (Matthew 11:28–30).

He wants us to learn from Him the blueprint for making the journey through difficult times.
This book methodically puts together and examines the comprehensive perspective and guidance offered in the Bible pertaining to temptation, hardship, and the trying moments that Christians are destined to encounter. Through a thorough exploration of these Biblical principles, it aims to provide a framework for understanding and effectively managing the challenges inherent in the Christian journey.

It teaches us that difficult times are real and that there are reasons why we experience them. It instructs readers on what to anticipate during such times and also imparts guidance on how to effectively navigate through them. It reminds us that there is an end in sight for all our difficult times.

This book is here to show us why we must never break ties with God no matter what. It is here to show us why severing ties with God is a very dangerous a step to take. It is why I believe you will find it a great resource for navigating the difficult times of your life. It will help you understand why you are going through those difficult moments, God's role in them, and how you can remain a faithful Believer during this period of trial.

It is important to remain a pursuer of God in every situation because there is a reward for doing so. *"But My servant Caleb, because he has a different spirit in him and has followed Me fully, I will bring into the land where he went, and his descendants shall inherit it" (Numbers 14:24, NKJV).*

These and more have been enumerated throughout the pages of this book. Above all, ours shall be the Crown of Life for living to please God, and for remaining His pursuers in our times of difficulty (James 1:12). It is my prayer that you will attain your reward as a faithful Child of God in difficult times.

CHAPTER ONE

DIFFICULT TIMES ARE A REALITY

Currently—as I write, Ghana is grappling with and emerging from grave damages of controlled release of water from the Akosombo Dam. Due to the impact of climate change, there has been a notable rise in rainfall, resulting in water levels exceeding the maximum capacity of the Dam. Consequently, to mitigate the risk of dam failure, a spillage operation began to take place between September 15 and October 15, 2023.

Though a precautionary action, the water release resulted in a surge in water flow along the Volta River, causing flooding in low-lying areas along its course. Communities such as Mepe, Battor, Sogakope, Mafi, Adidome, Ada, and others have been adversely affected by the flooding, necessitating urgent attention. It is a difficult situation people in these communities find themselves in. Among other inconveniences, they are dealing with the pain of losing their properties to disaster.

Authorities argued that the displacement was an unintended consequence of the controlled release of water, which was necessary to prevent potential overtopping and safeguarding the dam's integrity. It is an emergency situation that has led to the displacement of many of our citizens.

Experiencing a natural disaster is undoubtedly one of the most devastating events that can befall anyone. In the wake of such calamities, victims may lose not only their possessions, including their homes, but also the people closest to them, and this can be a traumatic life experience.

In March of 2023, our entire nation was thrown into a state of mourning when a young footballer and philanthropist, Christian Atsu, lost his life along with 54,000 others after being caught in a 7.8-magnitude earthquake in faraway Turkey.

Deaths such as Atsu's are heartbreaking, but it is not an uncommon experience amongst families. Dealing with the death of a loved one is one of the most difficult and challenging experiences in life. The Bible says there is a time to be born and a time to die (Ecclesiastes 3:1 – 8). So losses of loved ones are inevitable, and at some point, everyone will grapple with the departure of a parent, spouse, friend, or family member.

Sometimes, the source of our pain and difficulty is not death, but divorce or breakups. Maintaining a successful marriage requires considerable effort and dedication. Unfortunately, we've witnessed numerous instances of marriages reaching a point of breakdown, and culminating in divorce. Divorce can affect the entire members of families.

We hear stories, and we have experiences firsthand that emphasize the challenges and difficulties that come with this significant life transition. Although we will do well to recognize that in some instances, divorce can be the best course of action for a marriage that is no longer working, the process of divorce is undeniably painful, and has the prospect of dismantling a family unit, which can be emotionally taxing.

Breakups are an inevitable part of the journey of love, and they can be incredibly heart-wrenching. The transition from feelings of love to something unpleasant is undoubtedly a painful, difficult experience. Sometimes, these breakups occur between ordinary platonic friends, and yet it is no easy situation. Social connections and friendships play a vital role in our lives.

They contribute to our joy, shared experiences, and well-being. The significance of human connection has been likened to fundamental needs such as food and shelter for a healthy life. However, friendships, like seasons, change over time. Some people enter our lives fleetingly, serve specific roles like teammates or college fraternity brothers, while others endure and become lifelong companions.

Knowing how to nurture relationships is a healthy aspect of human connections. As social beings, our innate desire for love and friendship is undeniable. These connections are integral to maintaining a healthy and fulfilling life. Coping with changing friendships can be difficult, especially when parting ways with familiar faces and adapting to new ones.

Yet, an inevitable truth about life is that people come and go. It is a truth we must accept and allow ourselves to make space for those who genuinely wish to stay in our lives.

We must be unafraid to accept and release relationships, and welcome new faces that may contribute positively to our personal growth and success. When you sense that the time has come to release a friendship, don't hesitate to loosen your grip. Letting go opens the door to fresh opportunities and new connections that may align more closely with your evolving needs.

Part of why moving to a new place can come off to us as a difficult situation is that we lose friends in the process. But generally, moving invariably brings about a sense of stress and discomfort, whether it's to a nearby house or a city across the country. The unknowns associated with a new location can make seemingly simple tasks, like grocery shopping or getting gas, feel daunting. Trying to familiarize yourself in your new territory can raise the level of discomfort, and contribute to the overall stress of the move.

Falling sick or getting injured also adds to the pain or difficulty of our lives. Accidents and illnesses can unexpectedly interrupt our lives, despite our efforts to stay cautious and maintain good health. These unforeseen circumstances can challenge us, and cause us to be dissuaded from taking precautions and living a healthy lifestyle. Recovering from injuries is undeniably one of the most challenging experiences of life. It requires adjustments both physically and emotionally. Learning to live with changes to your body and abilities can pose challenges that make your life difficult.

Experiencing an injury is a challenging change that can disrupt your life at any age. Whether the injury occurs due to a specific incident or in a particular setting, it often throws off your regular routine and daily activities.
It is common to witness frustration in people dealing with or recovering from various injuries or illnesses as they grapple with their body's slow return to normal functioning.

Many of us have tasted the pain of losing a job. It can indeed be a devastating experience, especially when it brings about the uncertainty of basic needs like food. Facing the prospect of spending days with an empty stomach is undoubtedly one of the toughest challenges.

Navigating the various stages of life, regardless of age, is not without stress, as each developmental change introduces new challenges. Each transitional period is a state of change. But as human beings, we typically struggle with change. Yet the milestones throughout our lifetimes continuously prompt adjustments. We do not even stop to consider the process, notice opportunities our current life stage may present, and ride the wave of life with an open heart.

Instead, we are more inclined to focus on the challenges posed by growing older—gray hair, wrinkles, declining health, and the diminishing ability to perform tasks once executed with ease. There is no cure for the inevitability of aging. It is a shared human experience, and if we are fortunate enough to live long lives, aging becomes an integral part of our existence.

As we progress through the various stages of life, both our physical and mental states undergo transformations.
It's a natural part of aging to question and seek understanding about the changes occurring within and around us.

Following adolescence, particularly during our early 20s to early 30s, we encounter a crucial period where choices are made to navigate societal expectations. Sometimes, crisis in life begin to hit us right at this quarter life phase and can progress into midlife. The abundance of uncertainty and societal pressures during these times of crisis may contribute to feelings of confusion, and in more severe cases, may lead to conditions such as depression or even self-harm tendencies.

Life is not without its failures. Facing failure presents a difficult time to our lives. It is challenging, and touches various aspects of our lives. Sometimes, we fall short of goals we've dedicated ourselves to achieving. And this can evoke negative feelings—such as worthlessness, accompanied by a wave of negativity that can be difficult to endure. The emotional toll of failure is real and can cast a shadow on our journey.

The list of examples of the reality of difficult times can go on and on. What they all point to is that, life is full of challenging situations that can be difficult to deal with.

We all face these unexpected obstacles that often induce more stress than necessary. Life is a series of fluctuations—ups and downs, highs and lows, moments of joy and sorrow, and they are as constant as day and night.

Unlike the pleasant side of life, life's painful events and inevitable difficult situations require us to prepare to handle them in a manner that may lessen how deeply an effect they can have on us.

These difficult moments of life can disrupt our entire lives. But such is life as God wills. The Bible didn't promise that life would not be difficult. God didn't promise a life devoid of challenges; instead, He assured us that He would be by our side through it all, orchestrating every circumstance for our ultimate good (Isaiah 41:10; Romans 8:28).
This means, as Christians, we are not without hope. Each of these challenges listed above can become an opportunity for

building a God-glorifying life. No matter our situation, God can use them to our advantage.

Many of these formidable situations are beyond our control; we can only accept them, and devise a logical approach to handling them. The key is to glean positive outcomes from everything life throws our way. If we can maintain the right attitude towards life, our journey of pain can become easier to deal with.

Amidst these hardships, we've encountered numerous stories of success emerging from failure. Stories that highlight the rewards of patience and perseverance and a positive perspective. What do I mean? While the aftermath of natural disasters is undoubtedly challenging, we have the capacity to rise above such hardships and rebuild.

The human spirit is remarkably resilient, and even in the face of the toughest times, people find the strength to bounce back. Surviving a calamity offers us a second chance at rebuilding and starting anew. Amid the despair that follows natural disasters, a sense of community and mutual support often emerges. Helping one another becomes a crucial aspect of the recovery process. It is during these times that people find hope in shared strength, compassion, and the determination to overcome.

In the aftermath of a job loss, it is natural to feel a sense of hopelessness. However, it is crucial not to dwell on despair. Rather summon your strength and channel your efforts towards finding another, potentially even better job. Maintaining a calm and composed demeanor during this period is essential.
In times of adversity, resilience can become a key asset.

We can use the setback as motivation to explore new opportunities, acquire new skills, and enhance our employability.

Networking, updating your resume, and reaching out to potential employers can be part of the steps you can take toward regaining control of your professional life. If we remember that setbacks are temporary, and thereby remain steadfast in our new pursuits, we can turn the pages to a brighter chapter in our career. The secret is to keep calm, carry on, and seize every opportunity for positive change and growth.

In spite of the hardships associated with it, divorce can result in a positive change. Acknowledging this fact is instrumental in fostering the right attitude toward life after the dissolution of a marriage. It opens doors to new opportunities and allows individuals to rebuild their lives, learn from the experience, and pursue a better path.
While the journey through divorce is undoubtedly challenging, viewing it as a step toward a brighter and more fulfilling future can help individuals go about the process satisfactorily.

While aging is a facet of life beyond our control, how we approach it can significantly impact our experience.
Instead of viewing it with trepidation, we are being wise if we advocate planning ahead for old age to mitigate the potential hardships associated with it.

Pensions and retirement plans are among the strategies devised by prudent minds to ensure that aging is not synonymous with misery. Planning for financial security and well-being in the later stages of life allows us to navigate the challenges of aging more comfortably.

Accept the inevitability of getting older and prepare for it in order to cultivate a more fulfilling and secure future.

I need you to understand that setbacks are not the end but rather a part of the journey. I need you to view your failures as stepping stones toward greater success.

I need you to embrace the lessons here, and find inspiration and summoning the strength to persevere to eventual triumph. If you are facing tough times, keep your inspiration burning and go through the challenges with hope, faith and determination to overcome.

CHAPTER TWO

WHY WE EXPERIENCE DIFFICULT TIMES

ifficult times—why do we experience them?
There are many answers, the first of which is that
we don't know why! No, we do not know why we
have to go through suffering or difficult times. We
don't know why Christians—good people, innocent souls—
have to suffer. Paul expresses this for us: "We are pressed on
every side by troubles, but not crushed and broken. We are
perplexed because we don't know why things happen as they
do, but we don't give up and quit"
(2 Corinthians 4:8, TLB). So yes, there are no answers to the
question of why we suffer!

We often find ourselves without all the answers to suffering,
particularly when it comes to the hardships endured by Christians. To some, the primary cause of Christian suffering is our
fellowship with Christ, which is why we should rejoice in our
trials, rather than being taken aback by them (1 Peter 4:12).
It can even be asserted that Christians contribute to what may
be lacking in Christ's afflictions (Colossians 1:24).

But that's not all. Let's delve further into this mystery, perhaps we can learn something that will help our perplexity. First of all, the Bible says, "In the day of prosperity be joyful, and in the day of adversity consider: God has made the one as well as the other, so that man may not find out anything that will be after him" (Ecclesiastes 7:14, ESV)

For the purpose of this book, I will use suffering, hard times, difficult times, bad days, etc., interchangeably to refer to anything that causes us hurt or pain. From a divine perspective, suffering is a tool designed by God to prompt reflection and accomplish His purposes in our lives—outcomes that would not arise without trial or irritation.

By nature, difficult times are inherently painful. Going through a bad day or challenging period is challenging; it is never an easy experience. Regardless of our knowledge and efforts in applying strategies, it remains a painful process.

It hurts to lose your job and be broke. It hurts to be sick, lose a loved one or your relationship with them. As I indicated, experiencing adversity in life is confusing—it holds an element of mystery. Despite our understanding of some of the theological reasons for suffering as found in Scripture, when it strikes, questions still arise—Why me? Why now?

However, even in its mystery, suffering has a purpose.
God allows us to experience the bad times or difficult days for a reason, and it is not without meaning. For instance, suffering helps in the formation of Christ-like character in us (Romans 8:28-29). Difficult times serve as tests that challenge and prove our character and integrity and faith (James 1:2).
Importantly, our suffering provides opportunities for God's

glory, to be made manifest and for our lives to be transformed (John 9:1-3).

Most notably, suffering is inevitable in life. According to the Bible, the entire creation is in a state of pain and anguish (Romans 8:22). Our world is marked by sorrow and brokenness, and is subjected to futility by the very God who pronounced a curse on humanity for its disobedience. As a result, Christians share in the collective suffering and groaning of creation (Romans 8:20–23).

But I need you to note that suffering is not inherently virtuous, nor is it indicative of holiness. It is not a method for gaining favor with God or subduing the flesh. Ideally, when feasible, suffering should be avoided, as Christ Himself avoided it unless it conflicted with obedience to God's purpose.

Why We Suffer Difficult Times

We've all experienced good and bad times. When in bad times, our natural response often includes asking questions. Times of suffering, hardship or difficulty aren't pleasant. But they serve a wonderful purpose in our lives and in our relationship with God. Suffering is a divine instrument that serves to capture our attention, fulfill God's purposes in our lives, and deepen our faith in Him. In the midst of suffering, we are compelled to transition from relying on our own resources to living by faith in God's abundant provisions. This process builds and strengthens our reliance on God. The prodigal son is a perfect example. After squandering his wealth and facing poverty, he came to his senses and chose to return to his father. Faced with difficult times, he began to draw closer to his father. In much the same way, we have a tendency to pursue God when things get tough for us. Hard times take away our security and bring us to the place of realizing how much we cannot do without God. God does not want us to suffer or have difficult times, but when suffering occurs in our lives, He utilizes them for the purpose of drawing us to Him.

Suffering is at times the result of God's discipline, as mentioned in Hebrews 12:6: "For the Lord disciplines those he loves, and he punishes each one he accepts as his child" (NLT).

The challenging times we encounter may be a means of God correcting us. As a benevolent Father, God utilizes suffering to guide us back home when we go astray. God disciplines those He loves—which appears to be hardship (Hebrews 12:5–11).

In other words, our hard times are God's training school for us. As a tool for training, God employs it to develop our character and connection with Him. In this context, suffering is purposefully designed to lead us back to fellowship with God through genuine repentance after we have sinned in the past.

It also functions to remove negative aspects of our lives that tend to hinder our spiritual growth and profitability to God and His Kingdom.

God uses our troubles and sufferings to teach us how to help others through similar experiences. It is by learning through our own difficult times that we are able to empathize with and uplift fellow sufferers. To effectively prepare us for ministry, God takes us through a firsthand experience in suffering to equip us. In 2 Corinthians 1:4, Paul underscores that "He comforts us every time we have trouble, so when others have trouble, we can comfort them with the same comfort God gives us" (NCV). When we encounter the comforting grace of God amid our own troubles, it positions us to assist others in finding the same grace in their struggles. It is one reason God allows difficult times to hit us.

Suffering is a consequence of sin. A lot of the times, the hard times we face in life are the result of sin. Sin entered the world through Adam and Eve. We live in a fallen world. A world broken due to sin. As such, natural disasters, sicknesses, and other challenges occur as part of us having to live in this fallen world (Romans 8:22). The Bible makes us understand that we suffer as a direct outcome of the fall, a repercussion of human disobedience to God (Romans 5:12; 1 Corinthians 15:21).

The presence of suffering in our lives is a manifestation of living in a fractured world. Some suffering results from our own sinful and erroneous choices, while other aspects stem from the fallen nature of the world itself. This dimension of suffering should instill in us a deep yearning for a superior world—a world redeemed and liberated from sin—a world that God will ultimately establish upon His return.

The Bible says that we reap what we sow. So, our choices—inherently sinful, results in suffering. When David sinned by committing adultery with Uriah's wife and plotting Uriah's death in order to covet his wife, God punished him severely. When Eli's sons sinned against God, He wiped them all out.

God sometimes sends suffering or hardship to test our faith. Challenges and hardships can serve a purpose in the development and refinement of our faith. Throughout the Bible, we find the idea of God allowing or orchestrating trials to test and strengthen the faith of His children. Abraham is one such person. Perhaps the story of Abraham and his son Isaac is the most well-known instance of God testing the faith of His followers.

God instructed Abraham to sacrifice his beloved son Isaac as a test of his obedience and faith. Abraham demonstrated trust in God, and was willing to obey God (Genesis 22). But the whole test was distressing for him.

The story of Job recounts the life of a man who undergoes severe trials and losses, including the death of his family, loss of wealth, and personal affliction. Through it all, Job remains faithful to God. In James 1:2-4 (ESV), we read, "Count it all joy, my brothers, when you meet trials of various kinds, for you know that the testing of your faith produces steadfastness. And let steadfastness have its full effect, that you may be perfect and complete, lacking in nothing." This passage teaches us that our trials or difficult times can contribute to the maturation and completeness of our faith.

When God tests our faith through challenges, He does not intend for them to be arbitrary but to serve a purpose in shaping our character and faith. It is why we must persevere in faith during times of adversity.

There is something as "suffering for righteousness sake"
(2 Timothy 3:12). Not all forms of suffering can be attributed to our own mistakes, sin or foolishness. In many instances, we can find ourselves in the midst of hardship precisely because of our commitment to following Christ .Choosing to follow Christ can bring about various challenges and tribulations.

These difficulties arise not from personal wrongdoing but rather from conflicts that can emerge because our life does not align with the world. The Bible acknowledges that we would encounter trials and persecution as a consequence of our faithfulness to Christ. Jesus forewarned us about the potential adversities we might face for choosing to walk in His footsteps.

In Matthew 10:22 (ESV), He states, "And you will be hated by all for my name's sake. But the one who endures to the end will be saved." The practice of our Christian faith is enough grounds for facing opposition and hostility from those who reject Christ.
Suffering serves as a potent means of humbling us and curbing the rise of pride in our lives (2 Corinthians 12:7).
The Apostle Paul himself experienced the necessity of such humility when he was given a "thorn in his flesh."

This thorn was a source of discomfort or challenge, and it was intentionally provided by God to prevent him from succumbing to arrogance due to the privileges and revelations he had received.

Difficult times play a crucial role in reinforcing our awareness of our human frailty and the imperative to depend on God. These challenging experiences act as a mirror that reflect our vulnerability and remind us that, despite our capabilities, we ultimately need divine strength.

Moreover, the trials that we encounter is a reminder that this present world is not our permanent abode. Times of adversity underscore the transient nature of our earthly life and prompt us to fix our gaze on a better, eternal world that awaits us.
In the midst of hardship, a longing for the world to come is fostered in us, and we are encouraged to set our eyes on our heavenly home, where pain and suffering will be no more. The hard times God allows into your life shift our perspective and make us less enamored with the fleeting attractions of this present world.

But there is also the point that God uses our hardships to prepare for us a "glory beyond all comparison." This understanding is founded on insights from Paul's teachings in 2 Corinthians 4:17–18, which states, "For this light momentary affliction is preparing for us an eternal weight of glory beyond all comparison, 18 as we look not to the things that are seen but to the things that are unseen. For the things that are seen are transient, but the things that are unseen are eternal" (ESV).

This teaching provides another insight or perspective into why Christians experience difficult times. Paul conveys that the hardships and trials Christians endure in this present life are temporary and momentary when compared to the enduring and eternal glory that awaits us. Thus this suffering serves as a preparation for a weight of glory beyond any comparison.
He makes us understand that whatever we are experiencing,

however unpleasant, are "light" and insignificant when viewed in the context of eternity. But my emphasis is on the preparatory nature of this kind of suffering—it is molding, refining, and shaping us for a greater purpose and glory that transcends the challenges of the present.

The magnitude and significance of the glory awaiting us far surpass the difficulties we encounter in the here and now.
The sufferings are real and impactful; they are a pathway leading to an incomparable and everlasting glory in the presence of God.

One popular scripture—Hosea 4:6 readily comes to mind when we talk about suffering as a Christian. In that scripture, the Prophet reveals that the lack of knowledge can culminate in disaster or suffering. It provides an additional dimension to understanding why Christians face difficult times.

It states: "My people are destroyed for lack of knowledge; because you have rejected knowledge, I reject you from being a priest to me. And since you have forgotten the law of your God, I also will forget your children."

Hosea identifies the lack of knowledge and a disregard for God's laws as contributing factors to the challenges faced by us, the people of God. Notice the parallel between the significance of spiritual understanding and adherence to God's principles. It shows clearly that one dimension of why Christians may encounter difficult times is tied to knowledge and adherence to God's Word. When believers lack a deep understanding of God's truths and neglect to follow His guidance, we may inadvertently expose ourselves to challenges and struggles.

So let us keep in mind that difficulties can arise when we deviate from the knowledge and wisdom of the Word of God.

The rejection or ignorance of God's principles can lead to spiritual missteps, relational conflicts, and a departure from the path of righteousness. In such instances, we could find ourselves navigating challenging circumstances as a consequence of veering away from the foundational principles that God has provided to guide us on the path of peace.

CHAPTER THREE

ARE THINGS GETTING WORSE FOR YOU?

Life is often difficult as it is fraught with many challenges and hardships. Sometimes, the storm hit harder even when we do all the right things—stay away from sin, pray, fast or remain faithful to God. You may be faced with the hardest financial problem when you are most faithful in giving or tithing. A problem may exacerbate even when you dedicate to praying about it.

The righteous not only experience suffering while they pursue God, but things can even worsen for them. It makes me think of biblical figures like Joseph, Daniel, or Jairus, the ruler of the synagogue. God was Joseph's top concern while he worked in Potiphar's household. He continued to be faithful, but nothing improved. He went from servanthood to prison.

By a careful study of the Scriptures, we discover that Joseph spent more than 10 years between the time he was sold into slavery by his brothers and the time he rose to power in Egypt as prime minister. And throughout that painfully lonely, barren period, as he tried to trust and obey God, things only got worse.

It's easy to focus exclusively on Joseph's heroic traits and accomplishments. We often miss or overlook the years that he spent in despair and silence—the suffering caused by his brothers' treachery, being separated from his family, the toil and hard life he endured in slavery. As if these were not bad enough, the wife of his master Potiphar tries seduction and successfully labels unfounded accusations against him which ends him up in jail.

When we look back, it should dawn on us that God was not punishing Joseph by letting him go through difficult times, He was preparing to elevate him as a deliverer or savior. It is why he had to go through those periods of darkness. He first went into a pit in the bush that his brothers had dug for him. Then he went to Egypt and took a job as a common slave. And finally, he became a prisoner.

He suffered everywhere. It is as if those difficult moments were necessary or a prerequisite for God to fulfill His purposes for Joseph. But the point remains that sometimes, even in doing the right things, we get rewarded negatively. In trying to obey God, Joseph ends up in the prison. He winds up behind bars while attempting to follow God. Maybe if he had cooperated with his master's wife, he would not have ended up in jail.

Apart from Joseph, Daniel comes to mind. His resolve to remain obedient to God landed him in the lion's den. Daniel is one of the bravest and most submissive figures in all of Scripture. He defies the King's orders because it contradicts the Commandment of his God. Instead of praying to the Persian king only for thirty days as everyone was commanded to, he chose to keep up his daily prayers to the God of Israel. His enemies reported him to Darius the king, who had been made to initiate the decree. They were Daniel's enemies and plotted to catch him. Daniel was placed in a cave of lions by the king. He stood the risk of being devoured by those hungry lions. It was his destiny for choosing to be righteous. Thank God his enemies waited for news of his death, but he was never devoured.

In Mark 5:20–35, we read about Jairus the ruler of the synagogue. He approached Jesus desperately seeking help for his dying daughter. Jesus agreed to go with him. On the way, a woman with a 12-year-long issue of bleeding touched Jesus' cloak and was healed. In the midst of this delay, messengers arrived, informing Jairus that his daughter had died. Jesus encouraged Jairus to believe and brought him to his house. There, Jesus raised the girl from the dead.

As in the case of Joseph, Daniel and Jairus, we can occasionally expect that things get worse rather than better in our quest to follow God and obey Him. What keeps us going during those dire times is faith in God's upcoming grace for us. At that point, we have to remember God's promises and draw strength from them.

For many people, it is common belief or experience that their lives began to be worse when they began to turn from their sins and seek righteousness. The more they fast and pray, the worse their circumstances turned. For others, it could appear as though everyone else is making progress more quickly than them. It is the same scenario between the woman with the issue of blood and Jairus'. The woman came from nowhere and took her miracle while Jairus experienced a delayed response from Jesus. You do not have to feel left out by God because you haven't received answers to your prayers yet.

Seeing others blessed while we wait can sometimes make the wait even more agonizing and prolonged. People we know do not live to please God as we do appear to be doing better than us. They get married on time, have children, secure jobs—generally just do well, while we wait and wait and wait.

Hannah served God and made sacrifices year in year out, yet she was the barren one. Her rival, the likely ungodly one, became pregnant and had babies. Sarah waited and waited for one long promise. Hagar came of age and bypassed her and had a child with the same man. You know why these stories are in the Bible? To encourage those of us who would share similar experiences.

At one point, people from Jairus' house came to discourage him. "Your daughter is dead, there is no need to trouble the Teacher," they told him. Like him, we may be tempted to give up on our fire. We may be tempted to lessen the fervor with which we approach prayer, morality, and the things of God. What we fail to understand is that God has a destiny and purpose for each of us. The same power by which Hagar took seed instantly is the same power that delayed Sarah's.

The Bible instructs us to knock for it to be open to us, ask and receive or be given, and seek and find. However, in practice, we don't always get what we ask for. Our prayers typically receive answers later than we are willing to wait. And it can be annoying when that happens. It prompts us to question whether or not God actually hears us when we speak to Him.

There are moments when it seems He hears and meets the needs of others but not ours. It gets tough to trust God, and in fact, a lot of people have already stopped believing in God during trying times because they believe He won't ever help them or come through for them.

But, just because someone else is receiving what they want before you or because you think things are becoming worse shouldn't deter you from actively pursuing God. Remain hopeful about God's plan for your life. Have faith that your prayers are being heard. And since you know that your blessing is on the horizon, don't be afraid—instead, pursue God even more.

When it seems that God is not answering your prayers, don't give up setting fire to your altar. As we shall see elsewhere in this book, there are strong reasons why we cannot give up on our faith. If Hannah eventually had children—and Sarah; and if Joseph eventually got released from prison and rose to the pinnacle of power, God will come through for you.

God may ask you to walk with Him for a while. His reasons may be unknown or may not make sense, but just believe and obey.

In any case, we may be wrong to presume that those who experience miracles immediately didn't have to wait. Did you know that the woman with the issue of blood had suffered that condition for twelve years? Hagar had her own peculiar challenges—as a slave girl with little or no liberty—including the liberty to decide the man she wanted. Do not give up when you don't immediately see the Lord intervening in your situation.

Allow me to reassure you today: when you don't let the successes of others derail you, the Lord will surpass your expectations. So instead of entertaining fear, stir your faith. Continue to persevere in your faith.

Jesus encouraged the synagogue ruler to not be afraid but to just believe. Take it as your own word. Do not be afraid, just believe. By the time Jesus could have time to minister to the ruler, things had grown from bad to worse. His daughter had died. Yet Jesus encouraged him not to despair.

He is saying those same words to you today. Do not despair, My Child. I know it is hard. But do not be afraid. Just believe. Jairus would have thought to leave the Master alone.

There was no need seeking His help after his servant girl had died. Go home and bury your dead. But at Jesus' instruction, he remained with Him. Don't break ties with Jesus yet.
Don't stop praying yet. Don't give up hope yet. It is Jesus we are talking about. The Healer, the Miracle Worker, the Deliverer, the Saviour! Don't turn away from Him.

The reason many people quit following Jesus is because they listen to the devil. He is the deceiver who discourages people from keeping their faith alive until God comes through for them. Stop giving the enemy the opportunity to divert your attention from the impending miracle in your life. It may be 12 years—of hemorrhage or in prison, but you will come out, you will be healed. Don't be scared to keep believing for your breakthrough.

God is preparing you through your trials or hard times. Until He is through with you, you will experience confusion and discouragement because it will seem like you are moving backwards rather than forwards in life. You will even feel like you should lessen your pursuit of the Lord and start to question His power or influence over your circumstances.

If things are getting worse for you, I have good news for you. Even in your darkest hours, God is in charge. Joseph went through all the difficult times but eventually he ascended to fame, wealth, and power. He was forgotten by those he assisted for a considerable amount of time. These hardships didn't make him lose faith.

Despite these immense challenges, Joseph never lost hope. He remained steadfast in his faith and belief that God had a greater plan for him. Through each setback, Joseph persevered, using his intelligence and wisdom to navigate through difficult circumstances. Joseph's life can be summed up in his words when he met his brothers in Genesis 50:20,
"As for you, you meant evil against me, but God meant it for good." This sentiment also applies to the wife of Potiphar.

Although not all of us will command powerful nations or empires, it should be the goal of all of us to emulate the qualities Joseph upheld. Whether facing personal trials or enjoying moments of success, Joseph's story should encourage us to maintain our integrity, exhibit faith in the face of challenges, and extend compassion towards others.

Imitating Joseph's qualities means pursuing faith, forgiveness, and an understanding of God's redemptive purposes—a legacy worth emulating in our own journeys. We come to certain periods in our own lives where doubts about our future may discourage us. We should remember the words of Joseph: God has good intentions and a purpose for all of us, for which we should trust Him (Genesis 39:2).

Jairus points us to the need to resist negative voices and ungodly counsel. When people around him suggested not bothering

Jesus because his daughter was already dead, Jairus chose to listen to Jesus. It is the habit we must cultivate. We should learn from Jairus to block out negativity and focus on God's assurances. By placing our trust in God's words, we can experience divine intervention and blessings just as Jairus.

CHAPTER FOUR

PURSUING GOD IN YOUR DIFFICULT TIMES

Life's challenging moments can arise unexpectedly. They can hit us anytime, leaving us wondering what to do. What does God expect of us in such times? Does He expect that we turn our back on Him when things seem disappointing? In this chapter, I am going to show you what it means to remain a pursuer of God even in your difficult times.

Being a pursuer of God involves maintaining fidelity to Him regardless of your circumstances. A pursuer of God maintains faith in Him even when faced with adversity.

The essence of being a pursuer of God lies in not turning away from God, not abandoning your faith, but holding onto it, and in not succumbing to temptations. Now, let's embark on a more detailed exploration into these principles.

Staying Faithful

When we place our trust in someone, we harbor expectations from them. This reliance is grounded in the belief that they possess the capacity to fulfill our expectations.

For instance, entrusting your child to a school implies the expectation that the institution will impart academic knowledge to them. Should your child not perform well in their exams, it can lead to a sense of disappointment.

However, numerous instances exist of students who, despite initial setbacks, have gone on to excel in the same educational setting.

Similarly, our trust in God is based on belief in His capability to positively touch our lives with His power. We invest this trust with the anticipation that He can bestow His blessings on us, offer us protection, and provide guidance to us in all aspects of our life. Yet, much like a school falling short in aiding a student's academic success, there are instances when our expectations of God falter. We entrust Him with our plans, aspirations, and desires, only to have apparent discrepancies in their fruition. We rely on Him for assistance in securing a job, or leading a fulfilling life, or finding the right life partner, or maintaining good health, or recovering from illness. However, the outcomes may not align with our expectations. In such circumstances—when our expectation doesn't unfold as anticipated, what course of action should we pursue?

When I speak of pursuing God in challenging times, I am referring to the commitment to remaining faithful even when it seems that God has not fulfilled His part of the agreement. I must say that staying faithful is one of the key things that God wants us to look at carefully. One area I witnessed the benefits of staying faithful to God was when I served as priest of St.

Christopher, Otinibi. As I stated in my introduction, the location was a barren landscape on the outskirts of Accra.

The people were basically peasant farmers who earned very little. In fact, many of them were so young—even children. I didn't know how I was going to survive with my wife. Indeed, it was at a time when my wife was unemployed.

But we determined to stay faithful to God, and dedicate ourselves to His work. Through our staying faithful to God, He saw us through. Through His guidance, our humanly efforts blossomed into a bountiful success. By the grace of God, living in Otinibi was something I really enjoyed.
I had a wonderful relationship with my church community who were very committed to the things of God.

This experience made me realize that staying faithful to God brings rewards. When we stay faithful to God, He rewards us. Consider personalities like Abraham and Sarah, Hannah, as well as Zechariah and Elizabeth—all of whom ardently desired children. Despite the prolonged delay in the fulfillment of their desires, none of them turned their backs on God.

Year after year, in the face of childlessness, Hannah continued making sacrifices to God (1 Samuel 1:7). Zechariah and Elizabeth never stopped worshipping in the temple of God. They persisted in their service to Him.

"In the time of Herod king of Judea there was a priest named Zechariah, who belonged to the priestly division of Abijah; his wife Elizabeth was also a descendant of Aaron. Both of them were righteous in the sight of God, observing all the Lord's commands and decrees blamelessly. But they were childless because Elizabeth was not able to conceive, and they were both very old" (Luke 1:5-17, NIV).

To these couples, the challenge of childlessness persisted for many years. It was their own difficult times as a family or couple. The striking aspect of their situations does not lie solely in the eventual intervention of God, but in their maintenance of a steadfast faith during the difficult times. Given their advanced age, Elizabeth and her husband likely quit anticipating the blessing of a child.

They must have given up hopes of ever having a child, but they didn't give up their service to the Lord. Gabriel's announcement must have come as a surprise, as they had resigned themselves to a childless marriage. As far as they were concerned, they were going to their grave childless. Yet they were not bitter towards God. They did not abandon their service to Him, nor did they curse Him or cease to acknowledge Him as their God. It didn't mean they were happy with their situation, but they decided to not relate towards God based on their circumstance.

Their story should prompt a reflection on our own readiness to maintain fidelity in our service to God even when our blessings seem withheld. How many of us are prepared to keep being faithful Christians—attending church, winning souls, and giving to God—if God withholds our blessings?

Today, many of us find ourselves disillusioned with God because certain blessings—marriage, employment, visa acquisition, or having children—appear elusive. This situation is disheartening because it unveils the true motivations of our hearts. Are we worshipping God for who He is, or for what we hope to gain from our relationship with Him? Is our commitment to

God based merely on the blessings we seek?

A dozen individuals have allowed the disappointment of their unanswered prayers to taint their faith and spiritual conviction. Marriages have crumbled, and vows have been broken due to the anguish of childlessness. Faced with prolonged challenges, some people have compromised their integrity by turning to alternative sources—deities, for solace, protection, or success in their endeavors. The pressure of delayed marriages has led some to abandon their commitment to purity, while financial hardships have driven others to compromises.

In the midst of our trials, what God desires from us is a love that transcends conditions—loving Him unconditionally, just as He loves us. He yearns for a faith that remains resolute regardless of whether or not our prayers are answered in the way we expect.

The call is to not discard our faith when faced with difficulties but to persist in keeping it intact. It's an invitation to emulate the resilience of characters like the apostle Paul, who weathered numerous tribulations and emerged with an unyielding faith. As Paul declared, "I have fought a good fight, I have finished the race, and I have remained faithful" (2 Timothy 4:7, NLT).

Persevere in your own faith journey, irrespective of your challenges or difficult times. Draw inspiration from great men like Paul, who faced difficult times head-on and remained steadfast in their devotion to God. Instead of allowing disappointments to eat away your faith, anchor yourself in a strong commitment to love and trust God in all things.

That way, you share in the testimony of those who have faced trials and emerged with their faith not only intact but strengthened.

The worst thing that could happen to a Christian is for him or her to lose their faith at the end of their journey. It is the gravest peril a Christian could face. The prospect of standing before Jesus Christ on the day of reckoning with a faith that has crumbled doesn't augur well, and should hint us to preserve in our faith until the end. Don't appear before Jesus Christ on the day of accountability having lost the faith that was once delivered to you.

The life and experiences of Job invariably comes to mind when conversations about faithfulness in difficult times are shared. Even when confronted by his wife and pushed to the brink, Job steadfastly clung to his faith, refusing to let go.

"His wife said to him, "Are you still holding on to your faith? Why don't you just curse God and die!" Job answered, "You sound like one of those fools on the street corner! How can we accept all the good things that God gives us and not accept the problems?" So even after all that happened to Job, he did not sin. He did not accuse God of doing anything wrong" (Job 2:9-10, ERV).

Job's strong commitment to pursuing God persisted until he witnessed the faithfulness of God in the midst of his trials. If, at any point, you've turned away from God due to unmet expectations, I extend an invitation to you to return to Him today. Take courageous steps like the prodigal son, and make your way back to the waiting arms of your heavenly Father.

A celebration awaits your return! Or perhaps, like Peter, you've faltered and broken promises you once made to God. After pledging never to deny his Master, Peter stumbled and denied Jesus three times in a single night.

"Peter replied, "Even if all fall away on account of you, I never will." "Truly I tell you," Jesus answered, "this very night, before the rooster crows, you will disown me three times." "But Peter declared, "Even if I have to die with you, I will never disown you." And all the other disciples said the same" (Matthew 26:33-35, NIV).

"Now Peter sat outside in the courtyard. And a servant girl came to him, saying, "You also were with Jesus of Galilee." But he denied it before them all, saying, "I do not know what you are saying." And when he had gone out to the gateway, another girl saw him and said to those who were there, "This fellow also was with Jesus of Nazareth." But again he denied with an oath, "I do not know the Man!" And a little later those who stood by came up and said to Peter, "Surely you also are one of them, for your speech betrays you." Then he began to curse and swear, saying, "I do not know the Man!"

Immediately a rooster crowed. And Peter remembered the word of Jesus who had said to him, "Before the rooster crows, you will deny Me three times." So he went out and wept bitterly"(Matthew 26: 69-75, NKJV)

It was a moment of failure for Peter, yet Jesus restored Peter after his fall. In Christ, there is the promise of restoration for you. It doesn't matter how far you may have strayed.

It doesn't even matter the distance. Christ stands with open arms, ready to receive you. Come back and reclaim your place. Resume your race, undeterred by the trials that may have momentarily separated you from God. Difficult times should not serve as permanent barriers; they should be opportunities for rediscovering the enduring grace and love of our Savior.

Don't Yield to Sin or Temptation

Pursuing God in your difficult times also means not yielding to sin or temptation. I may not be aware of the specific temptations you are grappling with today, the challenges that are testing the strength of your faith, or the threats looming over your relationship with God. However, regardless of the nature of these struggles, I implore you to hold fast to your faith and remain faithful.

In the pursuit of God during difficult times, the key is not succumbing to sin or temptation. An instructive example comes from the time of the exodus, when Moses spent 40 days in the presence of God. The people of Israel presumed his prolonged absence meant he was dead or never coming back. They turned their backs on God and chose to serve a lesser god (Exodus 32).

Regrettably, this tendency to abandon faith in the face of challenges is not limited to the Israelites of ancient times. Many of us exhibit a similar inclination today. When confronted with temptation or adversity, we discard our faith and give up on God. We quit church, quit our roles in church, quit praying, quit giving to support the work of God.

Consider the case of Peter, how, when he was faced with the imminent death of Jesus, he denied Him. Even Gideon, a figure of great faith, experienced moments of wavering when he questioned why adversity had befallen them despite God's supposed favor.

"But Gideon replied to him, "With all due respect, my Lord, if the Lord is with us, why has all this happened to us? Where are all his amazing works that our ancestors recounted to us, saying, 'Didn't the Lord bring us up from Egypt?' But now the

Lord has abandoned us and allowed Midian to overpower us" (Judges 6:13, CEB).

Demas was drawn by the fanciful things of the world to quit being a Christian!

"Demas has deserted me because he loves the things of this life and has gone to Thessalonica" (2 Timothy 4:10, NLT).

But I want to encourage you to demonstrate resilience.
In the midst of your trials and temptations, resist the impulse to abandon your faith. Learn from those who momentarily turned away in moments of weakness.

The pursuit of God during difficult times involves holding firm to your convictions, resisting sin, and persevering in your faith. Keep at it even when circumstances seem overwhelming.

The struggle with impatience during times of waiting is real for all of us—and God is aware. Sarah was eager for the fulfillment of God's promise. She succumbed to a misguided idea and introduced Hagar into her marriage and inadvertently causing marital problems for herself and her husband. Similarly, when Saul was confronted with the delay in Samuel's arrival, he yielded to the pressure of the people and took matters into his own hands, transgressing what was forbidden (1 Samuel 13:5–14).

The challenge of serving God and remaining steadfast in His Word during difficult times is formidable. In moments of pain, confusion, and doubt, the temptation to abandon our faith becomes more pronounced. Yet, we have seen that there exist shining examples in the scriptures that provide inspiration for those of us facing such trials.

We have seen how Job keep his faith through a period of profound suffering. Jesus Christ Himself stood resolute in His mission and faced the Cross. With his indomitable spirit, Paul navigated numerous hardships. Hannah, Elizabeth and Zachariah were confronted with the agony of childlessness, but they demonstrated patience and trust in God's timing.

In your difficult times, the key to triumph is in looking up to these exemplary figures, and drawing strength and wisdom from their stories. Instead of succumbing to impatience or doubt, you can remain faithful and find solace and encouragement to trust in the divine plan of God.

CHAPTER FIVE

WHY PURSUE GOD IN DIFFICULT TIMES

Maintaining your relationship with God often appears straightforward until you are confronted by challenging circumstances. We have an inclination to question God allowing adversity in our life despite our faithful relationship with Him. In the earlier chapters, I expounded on the idea that God permits trials for a purpose. His omnipresence signifies His constant presence. His being present is not contingent upon the nature of our circumstances. He remains with us both in moments of ease and adversity.

God is also omniscient. He has an awareness of all our tribulations. He has knowledge of our struggles even before they transpire. In times of trouble, don't presume that the situation takes God by surprise as it might take you.

God's foreknowledge occasionally leads Him to forewarn us about impending dangers. We overlook His gestures often due to our insensitivity to His subtle guidance.
In our challenging times, it is key to acknowledge that God's

purpose transcends our immediate understanding. His presence endures regardless of the trials we face, and by His comprehensive knowledge, He guides us through our difficult times. The challenge with us does not lie in God's responsiveness, but in our inattentiveness to His cues: we often fail to discern His promptings or warnings. So God is not at fault, we are.

In this chapter, I want to encourage you to continue to pursue God in your difficult times. Irrespective of the circumstances you encounter or the emotions you may grapple with, it is imperative to steadfastly pursue God during your challenging periods—and here is why!

God is faithful

Yes, God is faithful and trustworthy. You can confidently entrust Him with every aspect of your life—your career, ministry, health, aspirations, dreams, goals, marriage, and family. In times of anxiety and concern, you can find solace in relying on Him. Even when challenging circumstances invade your life, rest assured that God permits them for a purpose; nothing He does is arbitrary. In hindsight, you will likely look back with gratitude someday, when you would comprehend the profound reasons behind those difficult times.

God's faithfulness is not just a declaration; it is a demonstrated reality. He consistently fulfills His promises and remains true to His word. His fairness and mercy ensure that He does not burden you with more than you can bear.

"You are tempted in the same way that everyone else is tempted. But God can be trusted not to let you be tempted too much, and he will show you how to escape from your temptations" (1 Corinthians 10:13, CEV).

Therefore, even in the midst of difficulties, God stands as the most reliable and compassionate partner to have. Turning to Him is not only wise but brings comfort and strength in the face of challenges. In your moments of need, let God be your ultimate source of guidance, support, and reliability.
There exists no alternative refuge, no other dependable source to which you can turn in moments of distress.

When faced with personal difficulties, there is no superior option than God. Human capabilities may falter, and the arm of flesh may prove unreliable, but in God's faithfulness, there is solace and strength. Unlike human endeavors, God never fails

(Jeremiah 17:5). He not only comforts us in times of trouble but also empowers us to achieve the seemingly impossible. He enables us to endure and overcome the challenges we face.

God's faithfulness extends to meeting our needs. While it may appear that we lack certain provisions, God ensures that we receive what is necessary at the opportune moment.

This assurance stresses the significance of persistently pursuing God in all aspects of life. In recognizing the unparalleled reliability of God, we find reason to continually seek Him, trusting that He will provide precisely what we need at the right time.

Truly, the faithfulness of God is the cornerstone of our journey. Through dedication to His service, my ministry experienced His boundless blessings.

Our reliance on fasting and prayer led to divine manifestations, wherein God has graciously revealed Himself to us. As we fasted and prayed in moments of need, God dispatched individuals to support our endeavors and provide the resources necessary for the enhancement of our church facilities.

Time and again, we witnessed the benevolence of God, as He stirred the hearts of individuals to contribute to the advancement of our cause. When we had to put together necessary things before its dedication, God unfailingly sent forth benefactors to bless us abundantly with the funds for it.

The miracle of blessings permeated our church.
This stream of blessings remained uninterrupted; they point to the unyielding faithfulness of our Creator.
Anywhere I stepped foot, the mere mention of the name of

the church and the lives we were touching elicited generous support. Our community flourished as a result, with hearts won over and spirits uplifted by the divine providence we received. A lot of donations were coming in. The children were being blessed. Anytime we needed something, we were getting it.

Staying faithful to God is very important in the times we are. When we stay faithful to him, he will take care of us. Through the grace of God, we achieved significant milestones.

Of course, there were difficulties in serving in remote locales or outskirts of town such as Otinibi, but we persevered.
It is commonly held that assignment to such areas constituted reprimand or penance.
Indeed, the perception often prevails that one's posting to such regions is a form of punitive measure.

Yet, I attest to the mercies of God throughout this period with gratitude. I harbour no regrets regarding my time spent in these outskirts, and I made a lot of impact.

At various junctures, divine intervention served as a tangible evidence of what it means for God to be faithful. In moments of adversity, our recourse to prayer and fasting resulted in demonstrations of God's fidelity. His interventions often reaffirmed my calling and bolstered my resolve.

Such occurrences point to His involvement in my ministerial pursuits. Admittedly, my initial reluctance and discontentment were obvious. I didn't like being posted there. But then God used whatever I had for the furtherance of the kingdom. I just needed to be available.
Pursuing God has been a commitment in my life I have never

given up on. Prayer and fasting have constituted integral facets of my pursuit of God I steadfastly adhere to without cessation. People who encounter me often ask, "Is this person really an Anglican priest?" I tell them, "Yes, I am."

They are not being skeptical or questioning the authenticity of my vocation as an Anglican priest. They just think I am different—too passionate or charismatic in my nature untypical of Anglican priesthood.

I pursue God in a Pentecostal manner. Upon my relocation to Osu, my commitment to spiritual growth persisted unabated.

I initiated a prayer, deliverance and miracle service dubbed "Miracle Wave." We experienced the power and great manifestations of the divine. There were testimonies of the miraculous such as the healing of the sick and women receiving the fruit of the womb.

The COVID-19 pandemic would not permit us to meet in person so we convened regularly online fervently interceding and bridging the gap between heaven and earth. Presently, our commitment to spiritual enrichment has translated into weekly Zoom gatherings every Tuesday.

This virtual meeting or platform now attracts participants exceeding one hundred, united in the pursuit of spiritual nourishment and growth.

The God who came through for me, and brought me this far, will come through for you, too—because He is faithful

God is Merciful and Compassionate

The Bible says, "It is of the Lord's mercies that we are not consumed, because his compassions fail not.

They are new every morning: great is thy faithfulness" (Lamentations 3:22-23, KJV). Choosing the side of God during difficult times offers the sweet benefit of experiencing His boundless mercies and compassion. This aspect is of utmost significance, particularly in the face of potential adversity orchestrated by malevolent forces.

The adversary, given the opportunity, would spare no effort to wreak havoc and destruction. But by maintaining our relationship with God, we open the door to receiving His abundant mercy.

In some instances, the difficulties we encounter may be directly linked to our transgressions or wrongful actions as we have seen in earlier chapters. The challenges we face might be the natural consequences of our own decisions. Yet, even when God deems it necessary to discipline us, His approach is characterized by love and mercy. He watches over us with a vigilant eye to ensure that the adversary does not prevail or devour us in our vulnerable moments. The mercies and compassion of God give us guidance in our difficult times, and offer us reassurance and a path to redemption. Therefore, choosing to remain in alignment with God not only shields us from the potential harm orchestrated by external forces but also allows us to bask in the mercies and compassion of our loving Father.

The example of David in choosing to be punished by God when he was faced with trouble serves as a practical illustration of the wisdom in turning to God in times of difficulty.

When presented with three options, David made the deliberate

choice to face the consequences in the hands of God.
His decision reveals a profound truth: it is preferable to fall into the hands of God than into the hands of mere mortals.

"David said to Gad, 'I am in deep distress. Let us fall into the hands of the LORD, for his mercy is great; but do not let me fall into human hands'" (2 Samuel 24:14, NIV).

David's story reinforces the idea that, in moments of trouble, God is the safest refuge. Turning to Him becomes not only a source of security but also an avenue to experience His goodness and mercies. Unlike the potential harshness or limited understanding of human responses, God's approach is characterized by love, compassion, and a commitment to our well-being.

If we want to enjoy God's mercy and compassion, we must maintain our relationship with Him.
"But you, O Lord, are a God merciful and gracious, slow to anger and abounding in steadfast love and faithfulness" (Psalm 86:15, ESV).

Nothing is Impossible with God

This is Jesus' assurance to us all. It is a comforting truth to hear. It is a statement of encouragement and hope to all who look up to God. God is limitless in His capabilities. There are no bounds to what He can achieve; His power knows no constraints. Hallelujah!—see Mark 10:27.

In moments of need or difficulty, this assurance beckons to us to shed fear, worry, and discouragement. The message is clear: maintain your faith steadfastly. Whatever the situation may be, God has the ability to address it. There is no request too big or too small for Him. His capacity to deliver and fulfill our needs is boundless. Approach God with confidence, trusting that He not only can but will intervene in your circumstances. With Him, there is always a pathway to deliverance and fulfillment.

He has Great Plans for You

Yes, that is the assurance the Bible gives us. "For I know the plans I have for you," says the Lord. "They are plans for good and not for disaster, to give you a future and a hope" (Jeremiah 29:11, NLT).

It is why we should continue to pursue God even in our difficult times. This scripture encapsulates the divine intention of God for a positive and purposeful future for us who place our trust in Him. It is a comforting reminder that God's plans for us are filled with goodness and hope, and that He intends to lead us toward a meaningful and fulfilling life.

Be encouraged to trust in God's overarching purpose for your life, even in the midst of uncertainties. God's plans transcend any momentary difficulties you may be facing now.

Knowing that the Creator has designed a path for you that leads to a future marked by goodness and hope should stir you to seek Him always.

Encountering difficult times does not necessarily imply that suffering is God's intended plan for you. The presence of challenges in your life does not signify God's abandonment or a deviation from His principal plan for you.

God has a purposeful plan for your life, and your current difficulties do not alter or negate that divine plan. Even when circumstances appear daunting, the promise is that God's good plan for you remains steadfast and unchanging.

As stated in 1 Corinthians 2:9, "No eye has seen, no ear has heard, and no mind has imagined what God has prepared for those who love him" (NLT). The mystery and richness of God's plan is laid bare in this Scripture. His intentions for our lives transcend human comprehension.

The difficulties you face are temporary, and in due time, God's purpose will unfold, and reveal the extraordinary blessings and fulfillment He has in store for us who love Him. This a source of hope and encouragement for me during my challenging times—and I hope it is for you too.

The full extent of the magnificent plans that God has for us often remains beyond complete comprehension. Consider the remarkable plan that unfolded for Joseph, who, in spite of encountering imprisonment, ultimately rose to a position of great power. Going through challenges such as finding himself in a dungeon did not preclude the possibility of ascending to prominence. From Joseph's journey, we can derive solace from the assurance that adversity is not the final chapter.

A time of elevation, celebration, and triumph awaits us—and this affirms that the ascent from difficult circumstances is not only conceivable but inevitable.

At times, God communicates His intentions through various channels such as dreams, visions, and prophetic revelations. But these glimpses into His plans are often partial; they are designed to convey His love and concern for us.

God has given you glimpse into His will or plan for you, the responsibility falls upon you to patiently await the unfolding of the complete picture. That disclosure or revelation is a clue to what is to come, what will gradually be unveiled over time.

Patiently waiting on God allows the details of His plan to emerge, ensuring that His purpose becomes increasingly clear. This waiting period becomes a test of our trust in His guidance and a demonstration of our faith in the assurance that, in due course, the entirety of His plan will be unveiled.

He will Come Through for You
At times, our actions may lead us down the wrong path, and in His just nature, God might allow consequences to follow. The Bible acknowledges that God, in His righteousness, may be temporarily angry.

"For a brief moment I deserted you, but with great compassion I will gather you. In overflowing anger for a moment I hid my face from you, but with everlasting love I will have compassion on you," says the LORD, your Redeemer" (Isaiah 54:7–8, ESV).

The assurance remains steadfast: God will ultimately come through for you. While His anger may endure for a season, His everlasting mercies prevail, and in due time, He will turn towards you with compassion and extend to you His mercies. This reflects the enduring nature of God's grace and His promise offering hope of redemption and reconciliation.

God will cause all things to work together for your good
Romans 8:28 is a promising assurance: "And we know that God causes everything to work together for the good of those who

love God and are called according to his purpose for them" (NLT). I take this scripture as a cornerstone of my faith. How God divinely orchestrates all circumstances for my benefit is refreshing!

In times of uncertainty, I can trust God. His sovereign control over every situation ensures that nothing will go away.
He has the capability to transform even adverse circumstances into favorable outcomes. After being sold, lied upon, and imprisoned, Joseph was unknowingly embarking on a journey to the palace. This is because of God's ability to bring blessed purposes out of adversity.

All these point to the need to persistently seek God, including in challenging times. The full scope of His plans may unfold in ways beyond our immediate understanding. With God, hardship may be a stepping stone to unforeseen blessings.

In the pursuit of God, we navigate through difficulties with the knowledge that He can shape our circumstances in a manner that results in all things working together for our ultimate good because we earnestly seek Him.

With God, our seemingly negative experiences can be turned into blessings. From the story of Joseph, we witness how God can use the adversity and evil intended for harm to ultimately bring about good. Joseph's journey from betrayal and imprisonment to a position of authority bears witness to this.

In a broader sense, our own negative experiences can become opportunities for growth and blessings when God uses them to impart crucial lessons. It can be lessons of resilience, faith, or compassion. God can utilize our trials to shape and refine our character. Furthermore, these experiences can be a testimony to others in their walk with God.

In Isaiah 65:24, we read, "I will answer them before they even call to me. While they are still talking about their needs, I will go ahead and answer their prayers!" (NLT). Here is a God who not only hears our prayers but, in His omniscient understanding, responds before we even vocalize our needs. That is the depth of the relationship He has with us who follow Him.

His intimate knowledge of our concerns and the promptness with which He addresses our needs is overwhelming.

I take pride in His divine attentiveness and pre-emptive grace showcasing His desire to meet me at the point of my needs before I approach Him.

God is always at work, ready to answer your needs before you articulate them. Pursuing God in difficult times is an expression of faith—a demonstration of your trust and belief in His sovereignty. When you maintain faith in God while faced with challenges, it shows your reliance on His guidance and provision. Your faith in God is not only a personal commitment but also an avenue to please Him. The Bible affirms that without faith, it is impossible to please God (Hebrews 11:6).

When you choose to trust Him, even in the midst of your difficult times, you bring joy to His heart. This pleasing faith activates His response. It becomes the basis for which God intervenes for you, or manifests His power in your life.

In other words, pursuing God in difficult times is a reciprocal relationship—a demonstration of your faith pleases God, and in turn, He responds by moving mountains and working wonders on your behalf.

RESPONDING TO LIFE'S DIFFICULT TIMES

In the Book of II Samuel chapter six, the Bible recounts the story of King David's attempt to bring the Ark of the Covenant to Jerusalem.

The Ark had been housed in the home of Abinadab after it was retrieved from the Philistines.

But David desired to move it to Jerusalem, the capital city. He organized a procession with people celebrating and dancing. As they transported the Ark on a cart, something happened.

"And they carried the ark of God on a new cart and brought it out of the house of Abinadab, which was on the hill.

And Uzzah and Ahio, the sons of Abinadab, were driving the new cart, with the ark of God, and Ahio went before the ark. And David and all the house of Israel were celebrating before the LORD, with songs and lyres and harps and tambourines and castanets and cymbals. And when they came to the threshing floor of Nacon, Uzzah put out his hand to the ark of God and took hold of it, for the oxen stumbled. And the anger of the LORD was kindled against Uzzah, and God struck him down there because of his error, and he died there beside the ark of God. And David was angry because the LORD had broken out against Uzzah. And that place is called Perez-uzzah to this day. And David was afraid of the LORD that day, and he said, "How can the ark of the LORD come to me?" So David was not willing to take the ark of the LORD into the city of David. But David took it aside to the house of Obed-edom the Gittite. And the ark of the LORD remained in the house of Obed-edom the Gittite three months, and the LORD blessed Obed-edom and all his household" (2 Samuel 6:1–11, ESV).

Uzzah was a good man, and so were his intentions.
He loved God and the things of God. So when the Ark of God almost fell, he reached out and touched it to steady it. Yet God became angry with him over the good he did. God didn't punish him with a plague or illness; He killed him outright! The incident caused David to become angry with the Lord and afraid of Him as well. He decided to abandon the Ark in the house of Obed-Edom in the meantime.

If an entity should be "ungrateful" and reward good with evil, it shouldn't be God. But that is what it looks like here.
If you are looking at this story from the same perspective as David, you would be angry with God, too.

But was it right for David to have been angry? Between David and his men and God, who erred? Let's analyze the facts.

The Ark was sacred, and there were specific instructions in the Mosaic Law regarding its transportation. According to the Law, only Levites were designated to carry the Ark.

They were to carry it using poles inserted through rings on its sides (Exodus 25:12-15; Numbers 4:15). This method ensured that the Ark, being holy and consecrated, was not touched directly by human hands. Uzzah's mistake was in directly touching the Ark, which went against God's prescribed method for handling it. While his intention might have been to prevent the Ark from falling when the oxen pulling the cart stumbled, touching it was a violation of God's command. Uzzah's actions violated the prescribed way of handling the Ark. He died as a consequence of not following instructions.

But the question on my mind is, how come David didn't seem to know how to rightly transport the Ark? Indeed, this is one of the few places David is seen taking an important action without first consulting God. The text says David went with "all the chosen men of Israel" to transport the Ark.

We didn't see David seeking counsel or consulting with God before deciding to transport the Ark. Transporting the Ark—and on a cart—was entirely the idea of David and his chosen men, not God's. This action of David is in contrast to his earlier practice of seeking guidance from God before major decisions (1 Samuel 30:8; 2 Samuel 5:19, 23).

The parallel account in 1 Chronicles 13:1 details that David consulted with his commanders and leaders before making the decision regarding the Ark: "Then David consulted with the captains of thousands and hundreds, and with every leader" (1 Chronicles 13:1, ESV).

Is it therefore a wonder that David ended up violating the commandment of God—which resulted in the death of Uzzah?

Many times, we are like David. When disaster strikes, or when we get into trouble, we tend to get angry with God and wish to distant ourselves from Him. We frequently get upset with God over issues in our lives.

We hold Him responsible for our woes. After all, He is All-powerful; He has the power to stop difficulties from invading our lives. He has the power to make the people we love reciprocate our love. Or he has the power to cause us to never meet the people we regret meeting in life. If we went somewhere and got into trouble, we ask why God didn't stop the trouble or prevent us from going there. But what we fail to understand is that, God is always speaking to us and directing us.

Unfortunately on our part, we are constantly failing to heed what God is saying. We are busy following our own ideas and ignoring God. It is only when disaster strikes that we remember we have a God. That is when we run back to God blaming Him for everything. Beloved, this is not how we ought to respond to our difficult times. In this chapter, I want to briefly show you how God wants us to respond when we find ourselves in difficult situations.

Do not be Surprised

A sound Biblical advice for us when we go through difficult times is to not allow it to overwhelm us. "Beloved, do not be surprised at the fiery trial when it comes upon you to test you, as though something strange were happening to you.

But rejoice insofar as you share Christ's sufferings, that you may also rejoice and be glad when his glory is revealed" (1 Peter 4:12–13, ESV). Surprises can take a negative toll on us. They can elicit a range of emotions—panic, anger, confusion, and stress. Not everyone possesses the innate capacity to cope with unexpected events without being adversely affected.

God doesn't want us to go through these experiences.

He wants us to approach trials with a mindset rooted in faith. He provides guidance to shield us from the negative impacts of life's surprises. He says in His word, "Do not be surprised at your fiery trials or difficult times." It means you have to learn to master your emotions enough to rise above the initial shock, and to refrain from being overwhelmed by the trials that come your way. It means learning to detach emotionally and hold your peace in the face of the problems or things that have the potential to give us shocks. It means learning resilience in the face of adversity, being filled with gratitude and rejoicing in suffering.

Count it All Joy

God wants us to adopt a right attitude for going through our trials or difficult times. The Bible says, "Count it all joy, my brothers, when you meet trials of various kinds, for you know that the testing of your faith produces steadfastness. And let steadfastness have its full effect, that you may be perfect and complete, lacking in nothing" (James 1:2–4, ESV).

This scripture invites us to approach trials with a perspective grounded in faith and positivity. It encourages us to see beyond the immediate difficulties. Recognize that not all unexpected events are inherently negative. Trials may initially appear as problems or disasters, but they possess the potential to be blessings in disguise. A setback can stir a dormant desire, kindle motivation, and foster determination, and set us on the path to success. View your trials as opportunities. They can propel you to greatness–which is a compelling reason to count it all joy.

Make Hay while the Sun Shines

If you happen to be basking in prosperity today, remember to prepare for potential challenges that tomorrow may bring. Economic downturns and other unforeseen circumstances can catch us off guard. It is up to us to wisely plan and prepare for such circumstances. The prodigal son didn't prepare for unforeseen circumstances. His lack of financial foresight drove him on a reckless spending spree without savings or investments, until it left him vulnerable when economic challenges arose.

When economic downturns or seasons of unemployment come, it is usually not God's intention for us to suffer. Sometimes, he gives us the opportunity to enjoy an abundance and store up ahead of our uncertain times.

If we exercise prudence and stewardship over the resources that God provides, we will consider abundance today as the chance to store up for the uncertainty of tomorrow's lean times.

Before facing the severe hardships that befell him, Job had enjoyed the goodness of God. He understood that both prosperity and adversity have their appointed times.

So it didn't take him by surprise, nor did it make him turn his back on God. I am not encouraging you to anticipate or desire adversity, but to embrace a mindset of preparedness.

I am letting you know that sometimes, the grace of God upon our lives is there to see us through challenging times. Appreciate the blessings of today but responsibly prepare for the uncertainties of tomorrow.

Persevere—for Your Crown

We cannot escape difficult times, but we can utilize them for a good reward. We can transform our adversities into blessings. The Bible promises a crown of life to those who endure and overcome in times of adversity. "Blessed is the one who perseveres under trial because, having stood the test, that person will receive the crown of life that the Lord has promised to those who love him" (James 1:12, NIV).

According to the Oxford Dictionary, to persevere is to "continue in a course of action even in the face of difficulty or with little or no indication of success." In other words, to persevere is to persist, to steadfastly carry on, to keep going even when the path seems insurmountable, and to resist the temptation of surrendering to adversity.

The essence of perseverance is to let your commitment fuel your endurance and persistence. It is an act of resilience, a refusal to yield to the overwhelming pressures that life may impose. It is the advice of James for those of us facing difficult times in our lives right now. He reveals also that the Lord has a crown of life to present as a reward to those who stand the test.

The difficulties you encounter are not futile or devoid of purpose. They refine your character and test your faith to determine if you are deserving of a reward. Therefore, in the face of life's storms, let the counsel of James be your guide—to persevere, persist, and endure. It is only in doing so that you will weather the trials and position yourself to receive the crown of life, an accolade that the Lord Himself will bestow upon you. No wonder when Obed-Edom received the Ark into his house, his household was blessed.

Remember it Shall Come to Pass

T. D. Jakes spoke of his own journey through difficult times and said, "They came, and they passed. And they came to pass." He longed for a time when the challenging time of his life—"days so dark" would be over. It came to pass for him.

Having weathered his storms, T.D. Jakes could now look back and affirm that those challenging times indeed passed. You can be sure he is glad he didn't quit.

"This too shall pass" can be your story too. The scriptures have proved it. What has come will go. What is coming will come and pass. It passed for Job, it passed for Paul, it passed for Jesus. Yours too will come and pass. Believe it. Difficult times are not permanent fixtures but fleeting moments. Your current struggles are not your final chapter.

THIS TOO SHALL PASS

No, I didn't just cite one of your favourite Bible references. And no, neither Paul nor Solomon wrote these words. However, this phrase has "all the hallmarks of a wise Bible saying" as one Christian writer puts it. Although not a Bible quotation, this phrase does inspire hope for the times when we yearn for respite—our difficult times. For when we are in our difficult times, all we ever hope for, pray for and desire earnestly is that they shall pass. Be it a sickness, the pain of a broken relationship, lost opportunity, shame or embarrassment, or a period of lack.

I believe we express these sentiments genuinely; they are driven by compassion for our loved ones when we see them endure suffering. Other times, we say these words to uplift our own sprit. Whether to ourselves or our loved ones, these words provide encouragement when our spirit is fatigued.

These words are comforting because they remind us that whatever challenges we are currently facing—be they physical, emotional, relational, or spiritual—are temporary.

Those hardships will soon subside and consequently transform into memories long forgotten. Admittedly, in the midst of adversity, things may not appear that way, and you can hardly believe the storm will be over.

But truly, the troubles we endure, whether in the form of illness, financial hardships, brokenness, and the like, will ultimately come to an end.

Time is dynamic; it brings forth change, varied concerns, challenges, and opportunities. Life unfolds in stages.

Whatever burden you currently bear is a stage that will pass. A brighter day is on the horizon! With time, your difficulties times will indeed pass.

Renowned American pastor Robert Harold Schuller titled one of his motivational books, Tough Times Never Last, But Tough People Do. Pastor Schuller's insight holds true; with faith and endurance, we can surpass our challenging moments. There is an end in sight for our every challenge, and this perspective is rooted in scripture. My assignment in this chapter is to prove to you from scripture that your difficult times won't last too long.

Your Weeping is Passing Away

Scripture declares that crying or expressing sorrow during our difficult times is not perpetual; it stops at a point. "Weeping may last through the night, but joy comes with the morning" (Psalm 30:5, NLT). The Psalmist uses the morning to refer to the time when our weeping is over. It does not literally mean our hard times would end overnight, but it assures that an end is certain—and not too distant. Our weeping will end at some point—and soon enough.

The Flames of Difficult Times will not Hurt You

Passing through difficult times can burn like fire. Unfortunately, God didn't promise immunity from such difficulties.

He won't take them away altogether. He said we will need to go through them. "When you pass through the waters, I will be with you; and when you pass through the rivers, they will not sweep over you. When you walk through the fire, you will not be burned; the flames will not set you ablaze"
(Isaiah 43:2, NIV).

God doesn't eliminate the challenges, He guarantees His protective presence in the midst of them.

Fortunately, He assures us of His presence and companionship during these trials. He does not allow the intensity of the blazing fire to consume us. No, our difficult times—much like walking through fire—will not ultimately define or destroy us. It is another prrof that "This too shall pass."

You Suffer for a Short Time

Thus the Bible declares. We suffer for a short time—and it is true. "And after you suffer for a short time, God, who gives all grace, will make everything right. He will make you strong and support you and keep you from falling.

He called you to share in his glory in Christ, a glory that will continue forever" (1 Peter 5:10, NCV). Our suffering is temporary, but the grace of God is enduring. After we suffer for a short time, it shall pass, because God will make everything right. The assurance that the duration of our suffering is limited is a comforting promise. In the face of adversity, God's grace is comprehensive, sufficient to restore, strengthen, and uplift us. Our afflictions are momentary—they are passing away.

"And this small and temporary trouble we suffer will bring us a tremendous and eternal glory, much greater than the trouble" (2 Corinthians 4:17, GNT). Temporary are our troubles; they shall pass.

The Lord will Deliver You

This too shall pass because the Lord will deliver you just as He has delivered and continues to deliver all righteous people. Joseph endured betrayal, slavery, and imprisonment, only to be delivered by God and elevated to a position of power and influence. Daniel faced the lions' den with faith and emerged unscathed through the miraculous deliverance orchestrated by God Almighty. The ultimate is Jesus Christ Himself.

His journey was marked by suffering and crucifixion, but it culminated in a triumphant resurrection.

His victory over death points to the power of God to deliver. The apostles, who bore the brunt of persecution and adversity for their faith, experienced divine deliverance time and again. The stories of their experiences of divine deliverance by the Almighty God attests to the truth of the Psalmist's words, "Many are the afflictions of the righteous, but the LORD delivers him out of them all" (Psalm 34:19, NKJV).

Whatever your affliction, it will pass when the Lord delivers you. This promise is not bound by time or circumstance; God is committed to deliver His people from every trial and tribulation.

God will Save You

Jesus saves. He saves from various perils—danger, illnesses, heartbreaks, demonic attacks, the stings of failure, or the entanglements of sin. If you need saving today, just call upon Him. "As for me, I will call upon God, and the LORD shall save me" (Psalm 55:16, NKJV). Calling upon God is an acknowledgment of our reliance on His infinite mercy and saving power.

When you call upon God, be ready to declare it is over—because He will cause your sorrows to pass. Acknowledge that it is over, not in despair, but in faith, for the Lord, in His mighty saving grace, will cause your sorrows to cease. It is a proclamation that God's intervention is imminent; you are about to be ushered into a season where sorrows yield to joy, and trials give way to triumph.

Many Trials for a Little While

Another scriptural proof or confirmation that "This too shall pass" was provided by Peter: "So be truly glad. There is wonderful joy ahead, even though you must endure many trials for a little while" (1 Peter 1:6, NLT). Our trials may be many, but they are for a little while only. All shall pass, and we shall welcome the season of joy that is ahead.

In the face of numerous trials, there is a reason for genuine gladness. Peter acknowledges the reality that enduring trials is an integral part of the Christian experience, but he offers a perspective shift when he emphasizes the transient nature of these challenges.

While our journey may be punctuated by difficulties, setbacks, and hardships, we can be assured that these trials are not perpetual. They are but fleeting moments.

Beyond his acknowledging our trials and difficult times, Peter paints the picture of our future as promised by God—a future marked by wonderful joy. Joy that transcends the temporary nature of our trials. Joy representing a season of genuine happiness and fulfillment.

God Will Heal You

He will heal us. The Bible assures us that "He heals the brokenhearted and bandages their wounds" (Psalm 147:3, NLT). When we get into difficult times—those moments of brokenness and emotional wounds, God stands ready to bring healing to our hearts. He will heal our hearts and wounds. He will not let us die in those conditions. He is the mender of broken hearts and the tender caregiver who bandages our wounds.

He not only recognizes our hurts, but engages in its restoration.

God is not indifferent to our pain. When life leads us into challenging terrains, the promise resounds that God's touch is available and inevitable. God will not leave us to languish in the depths of despair. God's intention is to bring us into restoration. He does not leave us to wither away in desolation.

He ensures to support us so that we do not succumb to the trials that threaten to overwhelm us. This promise is also proof that "This too shall pass." It will pass when God heals us.

A Time for Difficult Times

Every event on earth unfolds with precision and is guided by an appointed time. Everything is orchestrated with a higher purpose beyond our earthly comprehension. From the divine point, they are meticulously ordered components of a grand plan. They operate according to their set times and sessions. This includes the times of joy, celebrations, laughter, dancing and all the good things of life, as well as the bad times of death, losses, war, sorrow, mourning, and tears.

The preacher in Ecclesiastes points to the fact that indeed not a single phase of life lasts.

"For everything there is a season, and a time for every matter under heaven: a time to be born, and a time to die; a time to plant, and a time to pluck up what is planted; a time to kill, and a time to heal; a time to break down, and a time to build up; a time to weep, and a time to laugh; a time to mourn, and a time to dance; a time to cast away stones, and a time to gather stones together; a time to embrace, and a time to refrain from embracing; a time to seek, and a time to lose; a time to keep, and a time to cast away; a time to tear, and a time to sew; a time to keep silent, and a time to speak; a time to love, and a time to hate; a time for war, and a time for peace" (Ecclesiastes 3:1–8, ESV).

There is an impermanence inherent in every aspect of our existence. Everything is passing. Your difficult times are passing. The world itself is passing away. All things—good or bad—shall pass away. And "This too shall pass."

What is broken down in our lives is destined for restoration and rebuilding. The devil's influence is broken. What he has planted in your life will be plucked up. What is causing you to mourn or weep will give way to what will make you laugh and dance. What you have lost would be replaced. In due season, you will find and keep what you lost or cast away. Hate will yield to the power of love. The suppressed and unexpressed emotions within will find avenues of expression. The turmoil (war) will cease and give way to peace.

The challenges we face, no matter how overwhelming, are part of the temporal things of life. Afflictions, trials, and tribulations are passing; they will give way to moments of relief and joy. Whatever is currently eating away at us, killing us with distress, or sowing despair in us will inevitably pass.

In the present moment, you may find yourself diligently sewing and planting the seeds of your aspirations, investing time, energy, and passion to cultivate success or bring forth a cherished dream. However arduous this process might be, a shift is coming, a day of harvesting and joy.

That day will dawn when the toil of sewing in tears will conclude, giving way to a joyous celebration of the fruition of your dreams and a bountiful harvest of your efforts. The tears shed in the process will be covered by the radiant smiles that will accompany the realization of your aspirations.

Today may feel like the foundation stones are scattered, but a time of gathering is coming. It is destined to follow this phase. The challenges you face and the setbacks you endure are the building blocks for a stronger, more resilient foundation.
Every stumble, every hardship, contributes to the groundwork for future successes. The scattering may not be a sign of defeat but a precursor to a more solid future.

CHAPTER EIGHT

ENDURE–NOT SUCCUMB

The whole essence of this chapter is summed up in the experiences of two kings of Judah. Both of these kings faced difficult times during the time of their reigns, but they took contrasting approaches to them, resulting in markedly different outcomes. Allow me to introduce to you King Ahaz and King Manasseh, whose responses to adversity hold a very important lesson for us.

King Ahaz reigned over the southern kingdom of Judah, and faced various crises during his reign, including military threats from neighboring nations and internal challenges. Ahaz responded to these difficult times by becoming even more unfaithful to God. The Bible records that "In the time of his distress he became yet more faithless to the Lord—this same King Ahaz" (2 Chronicles 28:22, ESV).

Ahaz abandoned commitment to God's commands and principles. He did not use his challenges as an opportunity to draw closer to God or seek His guidance. He allowed his troubles to lead him further into unfaithfulness.

Many years later, Manasseh also became king over the southern kingdom of Judah. His reign is described as one of the most wicked periods in the history of Judah. Manasseh led the people into idolatry and disobedience to God. As a consequence of the disobedience, God allowed the king of Assyria to invade Judah. Manasseh was captured, humiliated by being bound with shackles and a hook put in his nose, and taken to Babylon.

"And when he was in distress, he entreated the favor of the LORD his God and humbled himself greatly before the God of his fathers. He prayed to him, and God was moved by his entreaty and heard his plea and brought him again to Jerusalem into his kingdom. Then Manasseh knew that the LORD was God" (2 Chronicles 33:12–13, ESV).

When he realized he was plunged into distress and captivity, Manasseh decided to turn to the Lord. He humbled himself greatly, seeking God's favor and forgiveness. He prayed earnestly, and the Lord, moved by his sincere entreaty, listened to his plea. Two different personalities, similar circumstances, but diverging approaches to them. I will classify today's Christians into either of these categories. We are either like Ahaz—falling more and more into sin in the face of difficulty or challenges, or we are like Manasseh, utilizing our difficult times as opportunities for drawing closer to God.

There are many Christians today who have the tendency to behave like Ahaz. When things are difficult for them, they turn away from God and seek solace, protection and help in lesser gods.
Going through difficult times is like going through the valley of the shadow of death. It presents outcomes that can either be positive or negative, beneficial or detrimental. For Christians,

adversities can point us to Jesus and help us build a deeper connection with Him. But they can also ruin our faith and let us into a shipwreck. Difficult times may manifest as temptations to deviate from God's will—where we find it difficult to obey God. Figures like Moses and Jonah disobeyed God, and faced consequences for it. Moses struck the rock instead of speaking to it, and was refused entry into the Promised Land.

Jonah encountered storms due to his reluctance to obey divine instructions. Peter's hard times came in the form of facing death. He was overpowered by fear and denied Jesus. To deny your Master in times of difficulty is a big failure, but that was Peter's story. Yet, thankfully, he received restoration.

I have extensively discussed how God orchestrates a purpose within our difficult times. However, the devil can also exploit our challenging periods for his malevolent objectives. He can capitalize upon our struggles to dismantle our faith and create a rift between us and God. That is what makes going through difficult times dangerous for the Believer.

Difficult times possess the potential to profoundly shake the foundations of our faith. When God wasn't coming through for the people of Israel, they succumbed to despair. Gideon spoke their mind during that period of God's silence: "And the angel of the LORD appeared to him and said to him,

"The LORD is with you, O mighty man of valor." And Gideon said to him, "Please, my lord, if the LORD is with us, why then has all this happened to us? And where are all his wonderful deeds that our fathers recounted to us, saying, 'Did not the LORD bring us up from Egypt?' But now the LORD has forsaken us and given us into the hand of Midian" (Judges 6:12-

13, ESV). Gideon struggled to believe and trust God in those times of national difficulty. Next is Elijah. Elijah plunged into deep depression before He could complete his divine assignment on Earth. He had achieved remarkable feats such as the showdown with the servants of Baal, but in his lowest moments, he wrestled with trusting God amid his challenges.

Similarly, John the Baptist began to doubt Jesus when he faced difficult times. At a time when the Saviour of the world, the son of God Himself was walking the face of the earth, he was held in the confines of a prison cell, awaiting deliverance that did not materialize. Jesus Himself warned that even the elect could be led astray, "For false christs and false prophets will arise and perform great signs and wonders, so as to lead astray, if possible, even the elect" (Matthew 24:24, ESV).

Even the most faithful can fail or fall. The chosen, staunch believers could lose their faith in the face of hardship or persecution. It calls for a cautious way of handling our difficult times.

There are two distinct categories of those who experience hardship: those who succumb, and those who endure.
The Bible says that hardship is meant to be endured and overcome, not succumbed to. "You therefore must endure hardship as a good soldier of Jesus Christ. No one engaged in warfare entangles himself with the affairs of this life, that he may please him who enlisted him as a soldier"(2 Timothy 2:3–4, NKJV).

Endurance is a virtue that transcends time and circumstance. It a force that empowers people to weather the storms of life. It is a commitment to persevere, to stand firm in times of trouble, and to go through our share of the challenges that mark the life journey of every human being. Endurance is not merely about surviving; it's about thriving in the midst of challenges.

It's about holding onto hope when darkness seems pervasive, about pressing forward when the path is steep and rugged (Romans 5:3-4).

Endurance transcends mere survival; it denotes the capacity to persist in the same manner as before the onset of suffering. For instance, amidst his numerous trials, the apostle Paul never reached a point where he conceded defeat, ceased his obedience to God, or abandoned the work for the cause of Christ.
Thus his endurance was never compromised. If bitterness, anger, or retaliation characterized our response to suffering,

we cannot claim to endure. Joseph suffered, but did not succumb. He remained faithful to God. Moses faced struggles in his calling or ministry, but he didn't quit until the day God called him to glory. He confronted plagues, the formidable army of Pharaoh, and a stiff-necked people, and weathered struggles that would have prompted many leaders to abandon their posts. Job persevered through difficult times and left an inspiring example worth emulating.

But not everyone who goes through difficult times emerges triumphant or victorious. Adam and Eve faltered in the face of adversity. They could not stand when the devil tempted them. They succumbed to the "lust of the flesh, the lust of the eyes, and the pride of life" (1 John 2:16, NKJV) and thus forfeited their idyllic abode in Eden.

Noah committed the sin of drunkenness and it resulted in problems between him and his children, including placing a curse upon Ham and his descendants. He demonstrates the vulnerability of even the most esteemed to personal struggles and the potential of succumbing to temptations and falling into many problems.

Abraham's journey through difficult times unfolded in the form of prolonged childlessness. Faced with the emotional strain of unfulfilled parenthood, he made the fateful decision to engage in a relationship with his wife's maid, resulting in marital strife and other complications. Abraham's experience illustrates the challenges that can arise when individuals grapple with unmet desires and resort to unwise solutions.

Samson, too, failed to recover from his fall. His difficult times manifested in the form of temptation with women. He perished alongside his adversaries, potentially at a juncture when God would have intended to further use him.

Saul also never had another chance after being rejected king for his disobedience. His rejection was final, and not even Samuel's intercession on his behalf swayed God's decision (1 Samuel 16:1). Saul's journey began with humility, but over time, pride crept in, leading him to turn away from God and disregard the counsel of Samuel, his spiritual father.

Solomon's story concluded tragically. He inherited a united kingdom, but ultimately bequeathed a divided one. His downfall can be traced back to his inability to stand firm during challenging moments, particularly in the face of temptations involving women and idols.

Judas Iscariot fell tragically and never rose again. The temptation with money proved a difficult time in his life that he never won. It led to his complete downfall. Judas' betrayal of Jesus in the Garden of Gethsemane demonstrates how a single difficult moment, compounded by poor choices, can have profound and lasting repercussions. What makes Judas' failure particularly disheartening is his proximity to eternal life in Christ that he forfeited for thirty pieces of silver.

Allowing our difficult times to breed disobedience can lead to a tragic outcomes, such as evidenced by the examples of irreversible falls from favor above. We can end up like Saul or Samson or Solomon or Judas Iscariot if we allow our difficult times to result in disobedience. Abraham and Solomon go further to demonstrate how the consequences of succumbing in our difficult times can impact not only our individual destinies but also the broader communities and legacies we influence.

As we can see, Bible characters are not always heroes. These stories dispel the notion that they are flawless heroes, and illustrate the very real and relatable struggles that we, like them, face daily.
These figures encountered moments of weakness and made choices that led to failure. Many of them failed in their times of difficulties, and teach us how to be careful not to fail by closely examining their mistakes and missteps. They prompt us to consider how we might respond in the face of adversity.

As I contemplate this generation's approach to the Faith, my concerns deepen. I observe a prevalence of attitudes similar to that of King Ahaz rather than the repentant spirit embodied by King Manasseh. It seems we are more predisposed to allowing our challenges and difficulties to lead us away from the comforting presence of God.

This is a disheartening trend that warrants attention and correction. Through this book, my earnest endeavor is to earnestly exhort and encourage and implore you, dear reader, to cultivate patience with God. Draw inspiration from the resilience exhibited by stalwart figures such as Moses, Job, and Manasseh.

Your response to difficult times can be a pivotal factor—either drawing you into a closer communion with God or, regrettably, distancing you from His sustaining presence.

I fervently pray that your story leans towards the former—an account of rising from the depths of despair, of refusing to succumb when faced with adversity, of preventing your faith from shipwrecking on the rocks of doubt, and of maintaining an unbroken bond with your Creator even in the midst of life's storms.

May you rise from your fall. May you not succumb in your times of difficulty. May your faith not shipwreck, and may your relationship with your God not sever because of your difficult times. In your moments of trial, may you instinctively seek the comforting embrace of God, and draw strength from Him rather than turning away.

May your journey through difficulties become an example of faith that persists even in the face of life's most formidable challenges.

CHAPTER NINE

WHEN YOU FINALLY BREAK THROUGH

It's been a long journey through this book from emphasizing the reality of difficult times, through to convincing ourselves that indeed, our difficult times have an expiry date.

If you have not yet exited your season of difficult times, rest assured that a time is coming when you will—you will be ushered into a fresh season where your difficult times will become a thing of the past.

Joseph left the prison, the Israelites got freed from slavery, God came through for Gideon, Job prospered again, Peter was restored to his position after "briefly" backsliding, and Jesus rose from the dead. Rahab the promiscuous woman became a faithful wife, and Ruth the widow remarried. Abraham and Sarah; Hannah; Zachariah and Elizabeth all had babies, and Simeon and Anna met Baby Jesus.

This final chapter is about when, by the grace of God, your difficult times elapse. Now you are healed or married, or have a baby, what next. Now you are employed, or your career or ministry is doing well, what next? Now the wait is over. What you desired or prayed for has been granted you by God, what next?

Preserve Your Blessing

On at least two occasions in the Bible, Jesus warned people to "Go and sin no more." They had come to the expiration of their difficult times, and Jesus was giving them guidance on what next. In John 5:1–13, Jesus healed a man at the pool of Bethesda. When Jesus later found him in the temple,

He instructed him to "Sin no more, lest a worse thing come upon you." (John 5:14, NKJV). It gives us clues to a connection between the man's previous condition and his lifestyle choices, so to speak.

In another instance (John 8:1-11), Jesus encountered a woman caught in adultery. Her accusers sought to kill her according to the Law which prescribed stoning for such offenses. Jesus challenged them, "Let him who is without sin among you be the first to throw a stone at her." After defeating and dispersing her accusers, Jesus dismissed her with the words, "Go, and from now on sin no more."

Jesus gave them this advice to guide them to preserve their blessings—the blessing of being healed and being forgiven. Jesus wanted to make them play their part in ensuring not to lose their physical healing, forgiveness and tree identities, so He emphasized avoiding sinful behaviors to prevent further harm. Jesus portrays that the beneficiaries of these blessings had a role to play in preserving their blessings.

Living in accordance with God's principles can contribute to the preservation of God's blessings in our life. Learning from these two, we can cultivate gratitude for our blessings and strive for moral integrity to safeguard our own blessings.

Paul also gave a very strong message to the Galatians about preserving their inheritance, breakthroughs and blessing.

In no uncertain terms, he wrote, "Stand fast therefore in the liberty by which Christ has made us free, and do not be entangled again with a yoke of bondage" (Galatians 5:1, NKJV). What Paul is saying here is that the Believers ought to ensure to preserve their blessing. He implores them to steadfastly maintain the freedom bestowed upon them through Christ, and to be vigilant and deliberate in protecting their precious blessing they have received in Christ.

In your case, it may be more than just your Christian liberty. Like the invalid man at the pool, your blessing or breakthrough may be your deliverance from your difficult times. You had to wait on God so long to finally find a partner, or have a child or secure a job. You want to make sure that you do not lose this blessing. Your yoke may be an addiction or illness or weakness that Christ has helped you to overcome. You want to ensure not to entertain habits or friendships that will serve as a breeding ground for the things you have or are trying to get rid of. So your first responsibility after God finally comes through for you is to guard your blessings steadfastly to avoid entanglements that might diminish or dilute them.

It's Time for Ministry

Along our journey through this book, we discovered that our life purposes or ministries and other blessings can emerge from our experiencing difficult times. God can utilize our difficult times to expose or awaken us to our calling or purpose. We have seen instances where people like Joseph faced adversity and emerged with purposes (Genesis 50:20).

Rahab emerged from an unpleasant past in Jericho, demonstrated great faith and was rewarded by becoming part of the lineage of Jesus (Joshua 2:1-21; Matthew 1:5). Hannah endured the anguish of prolonged barrenness, but was blessed with a son who became the prophet Samuel (1 Samuel 1:20).

If you are coming out of a difficult period of your life like Joseph or Rahab or Hannah, you may have gathered experiences that can bless others if you share them. You may find that the experiences gathered during challenging seasons hold the potential to be a source of blessing for others. This may be the time to accept to be the ruler, like Joseph, because it is reward time.

This could be the time to impart wisdom and guidance to others, just as God has guided and taught you. You can become a coach and mentor, and offer lessons you have gathered on your way—lessons on navigating relationships, achieving success, and embracing God's purpose–with others.
Jesus charged Peter to strengthen the other disciples when he stood on his feet again (Luke 22:31). The challenges we face in life serve to fortify our own character and also position us to uplift and empower those around us. Just as Peter was tasked with strengthening his fellow disciples, we too are called to lift others up through our own experiences.

The lessons embedded in our personal experiences are a source of empowerment. We shouldn't only own these experiences, we should take pride in them. Peter's momentary stumble did not define him; similarly our challenges or past do not diminish our worth or potential. Thus be proud of them and make good use of them.

As preachers, when we tell people God has a reason for allowing these things into their life, they don't believe. But when you go through your own storms or difficult times, you emerge stronger on the other side. You begin to see the sense in preachers claiming there is a purpose behind it all, because you begin to see that they were a refining process.

Scripture reminds us that God is a Comforter, and His comfort is not just for our benefit but also for the benefit of others. God comforts us so we can comfort others. (2 Corinthians 1:3-4). Having weathered life's storms, we are equipped to extend a hand of solace and guidance to those traveling similar paths. Our experiences, like a well-earned degree, equip us with practical knowledge and insights that qualify us to operate in those areas.

It's not Payback Time
When we go through difficult times in life, there comes a moment when we experience the fulfillment of God's promises and breakthrough from the hardships that once plagued us. One day, God will finally come through for us.
When we eventually break through, one of the battles we will fight is the urge or inclination to seek revenge on those who may have refused to aid us during our struggles. Trust me, you will always have to resist that tendency.

It is not uncommon that while in our low moments, we will encounter people with the ability to help us but who will deny us this help or inflict more pain on us.

The Disciples denied their Master instead of helping Him to carry His Cross. People reminiscent of Hannah's rival or Joseph's brothers, may have mocked, betrayed, or turned their backs on us in our times of need. Upon achieving success, our natural inclination might be to harbor thoughts of vengeance against them. But hey, no! That is not what Jesus taught us. Jesus implored forgiveness. When He Himself faced it, He prayed, "Father, forgive them, for they do not know what they do" (Luke 23:34, ESV).

Apart from what Jesus teaches us, Joseph's story must challenge us to really want to forgive. If after enduring the pit, slavery, and imprisonment, he forgave his brothers who had plotted against him, why not us? As he forgave, so too are we called to forgive. His realization that everything he went through was part of God's plan must challenge us to reevaluate our perspective. What if, in our own lives, the challenges we faced were also orchestrated by God for a greater purpose? The question that comes to mind is, Will we, like Joseph, extend forgiveness to those who wronged us, if we understood that their actions may have been a necessary part of our journey towards fulfilling God's plan for our lives?